DISCOVER THE KEYS TO A CLUTTER-FREE, EFFICIENT HOME WORK SPACE

P9-CNC-069

- The "Toss or Keep" test
- The best location for a fax machine
- Why using a "work circle" can save you hours of wasted time and energy
- Which time management system gives home office professionals an edge
- The office supplies you should never run low on—and those you never need
- The best way to save bank statements and cancelled checks
- The features to look for when you buy a phone

LISA KANAREK has helped thousands of clients achieve fantastic organizational results in their home-run businesses. Her proven methods can transform any home work space into a professional office that works for you ... with less stress and greater bottom-line rewards.

> "Packed with specific, practical, and comprehensive advice, this is the definitive how-to-do-it book on organizing the home office."
> —EDWIN C. BLISS, author of
> *Getting Things Done* and *Doing It Now*

ORGANIZING YOUR HOME OFFICE FOR SUCCESS

Expert Strategies That Can Work for You

LISA KANAREK

Ⓟ

A PLUME BOOK

PLUME

Published by the Penguin Group
Penguin Books USA Inc., 375 Hudson Street, New York, New York 10014, U.S.A.
Penguin Books Ltd, 27 Wrights Lane, London W8 5TZ, England
Penguin Books Australia Ltd, Ringwood, Victoria, Australia
Penguin Books Canada Ltd, 10 Alcorn Avenue, Toronto, Ontario, Canada M4V 3B2
Penguin Books (N.Z.) Ltd, 182–190 Wairau Road, Auckland 10, New Zealand

Penguin Books Ltd, Registered Offices:
Harmondsworth, Middlesex, England

First published by Plume, an imprint of New American
Library, a division of Penguin Books USA Inc.

First Printing, March, 1993
10 9 8 7 6 5 4 3 2 1

Ⓟ   REGISTERED TRADEMARK—MARCA REGISTRADA

LIBRARY OF CONGRESS CATALOGING IN PUBLICATION DATA:
Kanarek, Lisa.
    Organizing your home office for success : expert strategies that can work for you / Lisa
Kanarek.
        p.   cm.
    ISBN 0-452-26833-8
    1. Office management.   2. Home-based businesses—Management.
    I. Title.
    HF5547.K29   1993
    658'.041—dc20
                                                                92-24106
                                                                CIP

Printed in the United States of America
Set in Times Roman and Trade Gothic

Designed by Steven N. Stathakis

To my husband and best friend, Gary Weinstein,
for his constant encouragement, insight, and understanding.

CONTENTS

ACKNOWLEDGMENTS

INTRODUCTION   1
Who's Working at Home   Home Office Organizing   Taking Control
Different People, Different Styles   How to Use This Book

CHAPTER 1: THE CHALLENGES AND REWARDS OF WORKING AT HOME   7

Switching from a Corporate Office to a Home Office   If You've Never
Worked in a Corporate Office   Setting Up Your Home Office
Being Your Own Boss   Setting Your Own Hours   Working Alone
Seeing Clients at Home   No Dress Code   No Commuting   Merging Your
Personal and Professional Lives   Letting People Know You Mean Business

CHAPTER 2: FINDING THE RIGHT PLACE FOR YOUR HOME OFFICE   18

Some Space-Saving Tricks   Sample Layouts   The Spare Room
The Guest Bedroom   Your Bedroom   The Living Room, Dining Room,

or Family Room   The Kitchen   The Basement   The Garage
Closets   Clearing Out Your Chosen Office Space   A Step-by-Step Plan
for Decluttering   Staying Decluttered

CHAPTER 3: ARRANGING YOUR WORKSPACE   33

Organizing from the Ground Up   Where to Begin
Choosing a Basic Layout   Refining Your Master Plan
Choosing Office Furniture   Cheap Tricks   Arranging Your Office Furniture
Using a Planning Grid

CHAPTER 4: BUYING AND STORING OFFICE SUPPLIES   46

Finding the Right Products for You   Keeping Costs Down
Storing Extra Office Supplies

CHAPTER 5: CLEARING OFF YOUR DESK   53

What Belongs on Your Desk   Organizing Your Desk Drawers
What to Do If Your Desk Has No Drawers   The Right Way
to Use Stacking Trays   The Importance of Stacking Bins
Putting Your Walls to Work   More Cheap Tricks   Use a Work Circle

CHAPTER 6: CREATING YOUR OWN PLANNING NOTEBOOK   69

How to Design a Customized Planning Notebook
The "To Do" Section   The Monthly Calendar Section
The Current Projects Section   The Future Tasks Section
The Client Status Section   The Ideas Section   The Goals Section
The Addresses/Phone Numbers Section   The Books Section
The Phone Calls Section   The Travel Section   The Expenses Section
The Communication Section   The Notes Section   The Reference Section
The Personal Section   Getting Started   Do It Your Way

CHAPTER 7: OTHER PERSONAL PLANNING SYSTEMS   90

Using a Spiral Notebook to Plan   Computerized Planning
Electronic Pocket Organizers   Using a Commercially Available Planner
Using Tickler Files to Plan   Using Your New Personal Planning System

CHAPTER 8: STOP STACKING AND START FILING   108

Working Styles   Paper, Paper Everywhere   Sorting Your Papers
Types of Files   The P-A-P-E-R System   Hanging File Folders
Interior File Folders   Labeling Hanging Folders
Labeling Interior File Folders   Setting Up Your Current File System
Using Your Current File System   Clearing Out Your Current Files

CHAPTER 9: HOME OFFICE FILING SYSTEMS   124

Two Types of Reference Files: Current and Older   Purging Your Files
Filing 101   Letter Size or Legal Size?   Finding the Right Filing System
for You   Alphabetical Order: What Comes First?   Alphabetical Filing Systems
Categorical Filing Systems   Numerical Filing Systems
Color-Coding Your Files   Filing in Binders   Getting Started
Troubleshooting Your Files   Toward a Paperless Business Environment

CHAPTER 10: HANDLING INCOMING INFORMATION EFFICIENTLY   146

Using a Postal Service   Mail Handling Tips   How to Deal with Magazines
How to Deal with Newspapers   How to Handle Business Cards
Keeping Books Under Control

CHAPTER 11: ORGANIZING RECEIPTS   158

Keeping Track of Receipts   Using Files   Using Binders
Using Envelopes   Computerized Recordkeeping   Sample Categories for
Filing Receipts   Which Documents You Need to Keep and for How Long
Tips for Dealing with the Internal Revenue Service   Using a Certified
Public Accountant   How to Save Bank Statements and Cancelled Checks
Tips for Making Tax Time Easier   Keeping Track of Petty Cash

CHAPTER 12: MAKING BETTER USE OF YOUR TIME   171

How to Make Better Use of Your Time   Habits That Will Make You
More Productive   Three Types of Time   Handling Interruptions
Taking Breaks   Balancing Your Work Life and Home Life

CHAPTER 13: THE ELECTRONIC HOME OFFICE   188

Telephones: Making the Right Connection   Buying the Right Computer
Choosing the Right Printer   Choosing the Right Software to Help You
Get Organized   Organizing Your Data   Portable Computers
Facts on Faxes   Copiers

CHAPTER 14: TURNING YOUR CAR INTO A FUNCTIONAL OFFICE   207

You *Can* Take It with You   How to Create a Car Office Kit
Files, Not Piles   Helpful Car Office Organizing Products
Your Briefcase: The Link Between Your Car and Your Home Office
Keeping Track of Mileage   Car Phones   Portable Fax Machines

CHAPTER 15: GETTING STARTED   218

Changing Bad Habits   Making a Commitment to Change
Staying Organized

RESOURCE GUIDE   223

MANUFACTURER GUIDE   226

INDEX   231

ACKNOWLEDGMENTS

Thank you to everyone who has helped and supported me throughout this project, including friends and family. I am thankful to the many clients I have met along the way.

Special thanks to my editor, Michaela Hamilton, who provided me with guidance and advice; to my literary agent, Denise Marcil, for her hard work and expertise; to Nellie Sabin, for helping to shape and enhance this book; to my parents, Joseph and Raquel Kanarek, who have always been an inspiration to me; and to my Uncle Sam Gardner, for believing in me.

INTRODUCTION

Corporate America is moving home. The work that used to be done in high-rise office buildings is now being done in kitchens, basements, spare rooms—even corners of rooms—all over the country. Computers, fax machines, and modems make it possible to do almost any work in a home office that can be done in a corporate office. This is changing the ways in which both corporations and individuals get things done.

WHO'S WORKING AT HOME

There are over 34 million homeworkers in the United States today. Everyone from displaced corporate executives to the President of the United States has a home office.

There are a number of reasons why corporations are more and more willing to set up employees in home offices. Home-based corporate employees save companies from having to pay high overhead costs. National companies are finding that maintaining representatives all over the country not only allows them to reach a wider talent base, but enables them to serve local clients better—and these representatives can still stay in close touch with management by means of electronic mail and cost-effective teleconferencing. Companies of all sizes are finding that allowing workers to split their time between a corporate office and a home office keeps talented employees (and often new mothers) happy, with a minimum of disruptions, which saves the expense of finding and training new people.

Added to the ranks of corporate employees who work at home are the ever-growing numbers of self-employed people, including consultants, financial planners, physicians, lawyers, entrepreneurs, writers, artists, and freelancers of all types. Some home office professionals have worked in corporate offices; some haven't. Some moonlight out of home offices but have a different job during the day. Others have set up cottage industries at home, or have started an informal, small business that is rapidly becoming bigger and more time-consuming. Today retirees are starting new, home-based careers; mothers are interested in working at home so that they can be near their children; and corporate employees who were laid off during company downsizing are deciding to set up shop for themselves instead of going back to the nine-to-five lifestyle. All of these people have found that maintaining an office at home beats paying high rents for space elsewhere and offers other advantages, which we'll get to later.

HOME OFFICE ORGANIZING

There *is* a catch. Running a home office is not like running a corporate office—or, for that matter, like running a home. My specialty is organizing offices and everything in them, and over the years I've noticed that home offices present certain unique challenges. The home office professionals who recognize and deal with these challenges are more effective and more in control—and therefore less stressed, less frustrated, and more successful at what they do—than those who don't.

I'd like to share with you the guidelines and recommendations I give my private clients and my audiences during seminars so that you can spend less time fighting meaningless battles with your papers and more time on productive work. This book will give you the direction you need to do the following:

- Set up an efficient home office you enjoy working in
- Reduce the amount of time you spend looking for things

- Increase your productivity
- Streamline the way you handle paperwork
- Take control of your time
- Increase your professionalism
- Focus on your priorities and goals
- Respond swiftly to new developments

In order to be truly productive, you need to be one step ahead of events, instead of always just reacting to what each day brings. By implementing the suggestions in this book, you'll find that you finally have the time you need to get caught up, to think creatively, to meet more challenges, and to do whatever it is you want to do.

In that the secret to making your home office work for you is to organize it and keep it organized, I've written this book to get you on the right track and to keep you moving forward. It's like having your own professional organizer with you twenty-four hours a day.

I can't organize you; only you can. What I *can* do is provide you with the tools and the information you need to get organized and maintain a comfortable level of organization. Although I have a lot to say about how to do things, I'd like you to remember that the point really isn't the process, but the results you'll get.

TAKING CONTROL

In a corporate setting, you get a day's pay whether or not you accomplish a day's worth of work. When you work at home, any time you waste will eventually be reflected in your income, whether you spend half an hour talking on the phone with a friend or fifteen minutes looking for a misplaced brochure. Your income is directly related to how productive you are.

As a home office professional, you can't rely on other people to help you with your productivity. You're on your own. The bottom line is that in order to take control of your work, you first have to take control of your office.

Organizing Your Home Office for Success is devoted to the special needs of those who work in a home office, and will take you step by step through the entire process of organizing a home office. You'll learn how to do the following:

- Find the right space for your home office
- Set up a functional work area
- Organize and store your supplies
- Create a daily planner
- Clear your office of unnecessary items and stacks of paper
- Design an efficient home office filing system that works for you
- Set up systems that help you keep papers moving ahead
- Organize for tax time
- Make the most of home office electronics
- Turn your car into an efficient traveling office

Even if you're already organized—and most of the home office professionals I've met are smart, capable people—I guarantee you'll learn new methods you can use to fine-tune your approach. Usually making adjustments to your working style is more effective than trying to make drastic changes. In that keeping up with the latest office products is part of my job, you'll also learn about some helpful items you may never have known existed.

For those of you who are ashamed of your home office because it's such a mess, take heart: you've come to the right book. No matter how bad you think your office is, I've seen worse. One client actually hired me because she was afraid of what others would think of her if she died suddenly and they discovered what her desk looked like! She was ashamed of how disorganized she was and, on a deeper level, felt ineffectual and out of control. Fortunately we were able to get her on track and she lived to enjoy the benefits of an organized home office.

This book is not about how to start or run a home-based business. There are several good books that cover that topic in detail. Instead, I'll show you organizing methods that every home office professional can apply to his or her work in order to become more efficient, more productive, and more successful.

DIFFERENT PEOPLE, DIFFERENT STYLES

Corporate offices are always somewhat alike, but home offices are as varied as they can be. Your home office reflects your style and personality, and while it makes sense to you, it might drive someone else crazy. Similarly, an organizational method that works for you could be totally inappropriate for someone else. For this reason, I always give you options from which to choose. If you're the type of person who uses a free-association approach to filing (like my client who had a When I Feel Like It file), don't bother trying to implement the numerical filing system presented in Chapter 9. However, if you prefer a consistent, predictable filing system with no surprises, the numerical approach could be perfect for you.

I don't like to take a rigid approach to anything, and I don't always agree with what other experts have to say. For example, it's often said that you should handle each piece of paper just once. If you act on it right away, the theory goes, you'll get more done, and papers won't be around long enough to clutter up your life. But how reasonable is this? In my view, not very. It sounds good, but it doesn't work. I'm only going to suggest proven methods that have worked for my clients and that can work for you, too.

Being a neatnik actually has nothing to do with being efficient. Although I am compulsively tidy, I'm not going to tell you that you have to empty out your junk drawer or line up your pencils from shortest to longest. Being a perfectionist is counterproductive because obsessing over details takes time away from working. Although I do want you to get organized, my goal is to show you how to stay focused on your work and spend a minimum of time on nonsense.

HOW TO USE THIS BOOK

I guess authors always hope readers will read their book from beginning to end, and I'm no exception. However, if you must dip into just the sections you think you need, I hope you'll at least skim the rest of the book, because you never know where you'll find a tip that will work for you. After you have read and used this book, it should be dog-eared, marked, and highlighted. That's the only way you're going to get completely organized.

I hope that once you get started, you'll continue to reinforce what you should be doing by referring to the book later. I've used lists and numbered steps wherever possible so that you can read and review the book quickly.

Each chapter of *Organizing Your Home Office for Success* is dedicated to a particular aspect of organizing that is important to home office professionals. In addition, I've included a resource guide and product guide at the back of the book that will direct you to sources of further information.

If you want to get organized or be better organized, you can do it. Clients of mine whose offices weren't under control have been amazed at their new level of productivity after becoming organized. Many have said they wondered how they ever functioned before. Getting organized is a lot like changing to a healthy diet or getting onto a household budget: once you've made it a habit, it becomes easy to maintain.

So let's get started, and before you know it, you won't recognize your own office. In fact, I recommend that you take a picture of your office (or soon-to-be office) now and another when you've finished. The difference between the way it looks now and the way it will look after you've finished organizing it will astonish you!

1

THE CHALLENGES
AND REWARDS
OF WORKING
AT HOME

When people find out that I work out of my home, they often say, "Oh, that sounds like fun!" or, "I wish I could do that." And I usually find myself answering, "Yes, it's fun, *but ...*"

Like anything else, working at home has both advantages and challenges. Many aspects of working at home work both ways, with both a pleasant side and a downside. By implementing some special organizing methods that work for home office professionals, you can maximize the advantages and meet the challenges of a home office successfully.

This chapter will alert you to some of the special considerations that are part of working at home. Throughout the rest of the book, we'll find out how to effectively handle each one.

SWITCHING FROM A CORPORATE OFFICE TO A HOME OFFICE

Advantage: You're independent.

Challenge: You have none of the support services of a job in a corporate office.

Working at home is not at all like working in a corporate office. If you're switching from a corporate setting to a home office, first spend some time analyzing the biggest conveniences of your corporate arrangement. What are you really going to miss about it? In what ways does the corporate setting work for you? How are you going to compensate for those advantages at home?

When Janie, a medical representative, started working out of her home, it seemed as if she'd changed not only locations but personalities. In her corporate office, Janie had been extremely efficient and organized. Her desk had always been clear, and whenever anyone needed anything, they knew Janie would be able to find it in her files immediately. After just 30 days at home, Janie's desk in her bedroom was overflowing, and she had supplies and papers stashed all over the house; she was spending entirely too much time running around trying to find things and trying to find places to put things.

Changing your environment changes the way you work. In Janie's case, switching to a home environment meant she no longer had a spacious office in which to store everything; she no longer had a secretary to help her keep up with the typing, filing, paperwork, and phone calls; and she no longer had access to time-saving conveniences such as the "industrial strength" copier. Janie was having trouble maintaining both her standards and her pace.

When I first met with Janie, I knew right away she would have to find a better location for her home office so that she could consolidate her files and supplies. By putting a Murphy bed in the spare bedroom (see page 20), we freed up enough space for her to have a bona fide office. From there we worked on innovative storage techniques, using some old furniture in new ways, as well as some new products.

After her office overhaul, Janie was ecstatic. She had always been an organized person, but working out of a makeshift home office had overwhelmed her skills.

I've seen many talented executives undermine new home-based careers by underestimating how much time it would take them to juggle the roles of errand runner, secretary, receptionist, mail room clerk, and purchasing department head—not to mention sales and marketing manager! All home office professionals have to wear several hats, but those who are self-employed have the most demands on their time.

When Barry, a vice president of an electronics firm, retired from his corporate job, he decided to open a consulting firm in his home. Although he was well organized, had a well-equipped home office, had plenty of clients, and had the skills to be a consultant, there was a fatal flaw in Barry's business plan. He couldn't type. Barry had figured that typing couldn't be too difficult; besides, didn't he have a spelling check on his computer? To his dismay, he discovered that a single letter was taking him an entire hour. We found Barry a secretarial service to help him handle his correspondence and proposals, which not only freed up a lot of Barry's time, but removed a source of irritation from his day.

IF YOU'VE NEVER WORKED IN A CORPORATE OFFICE

Advantage: You can cultivate good home office work habits from the beginning.

Challenge: Starting from scratch can be overwhelming and usually involves making unnecessary mistakes.

Those of you who have never worked in a corporate setting are lucky. You won't need to change any bad habits, and you won't miss the perks. However, you also don't have any model to follow as you set up your own office at home.

Carol, a client of mine, has a creative flair. When her children were growing up, she would hand paint T-shirts and give them away as birthday presents. Often her friends would say, "You know, you really ought to sell these." After hearing this for the fiftieth time, Carol decided her friends had a point, and she opened her own T-shirt business.

Success came too quickly. Carol was strong on T-shirts but not much on tracking accounts receivable or preparing tax records. All she wanted to do was decorate a few shirts and make a little money, but almost immediately the "business" side of her business started to drive her crazy. We spent an entire week setting up a home office for Carol and designing a filing system that would help her keep her accounts organized. Now her paperwork is taking up much less of her time, and she is finding her business fun again.

QUICK TIP FOR HOME OFFICE PROFESSIONALS

Take the time to get organized. In the long run, you'll come out ahead. Many people find it hard to take time off from working to see what they need to change about their methods. This is especially true of people who are already basically organized. However, just as it takes money to make money, it also takes time to save time. Motivating idea: every improvement you make will have an effect on the bottom line of your business.

SETTING UP YOUR HOME OFFICE

Advantages: Low overhead.
              Freedom to furnish your office however you wish.

Challenges: Carving an office out of living space in your home.
              Paying for all of your own equipment.

One advantage of working at home is that you have low overhead because you aren't paying rent or a mortgage on office space elsewhere. On the other hand, you have to create an office somewhere within your home, which may mean making do with a cramped space or working around the needs (and mess!) of the rest of your family. Although you may need to be extremely resourceful, it *is* possible to set up an efficient office in an odd space or in a room that does double duty as something else.

As a home office professional, you can furnish your office however you like. This helps make your office an enjoyable place in which to spend time, and if you're in a creative profession, it may help you think in innovative ways. The downside of furnishing your workspace yourself is that you may have to buy all of your own office equipment, including supplies, furniture, and electronics. This quickly becomes very expensive. By making your choices carefully, you can get the most out of each expense. For example, maybe a combination fax/copier would be cost effective for you, or perhaps there's a special type of shelving that will fit that little space in the corner and save you the cost of a new filing cabinet.

I've found that most people who work at home basically let their office create itself. Piece by piece they add equipment—an answering machine, a computer stand, some shelves, and so on—until their office evolves into a workspace that suits their needs, but is less efficient than it could be. Using this book, I'd like you either to start off right with a comprehensive plan for your new home office, or, if you already have an office at home, to take a fresh look at how you might make the most of it.

BEING YOUR OWN BOSS

Advantage: No boss looking over your shoulder.

Challenge: Disciplining yourself.

It takes a particular personality to succeed in a home-based job. If you're a good self-motivator, you may love being your own boss so much that you'll never be able to work for anyone else. On the other hand, if you aren't willing to tell yourself what to do and then do it, I'd advise you not to try to work out of your home.

Every year, new businesses fail. This is due to a variety of causes, but one reason is that many people don't realize how challenging it is to be your own boss. I've seen very capable people unravel after a few months of working at home. Once they get back into a corporate environment, where they are stimulated by the presence of a boss and co-workers and have help and support from others, they are not only happier but much more effective.

SETTING YOUR OWN HOURS

Advantage: No time clock to punch.

Challenge: No regular schedule.

Good time management is crucial for the home office professional. Not only are you juggling all of those roles I mentioned earlier, but you are undoubtedly finding plenty of things to do around the house other than professional work. Often what should be a two-hour project can end up taking forty-eight hours to complete. Working your own hours at your own pace is fine, until the amount of work you produce drops. By disciplining yourself and getting on a regular schedule, you can still be productive while enjoying the benefits of working at home.

Self-employed home office professionals have the satisfaction of running their own business and watching it grow through the results of their own efforts. They also bear full responsibility for all of the problems, deadlines, and bills. If you're not on someone else's payroll, time is truly money. Each interruption and wasted hour translates into less work accomplished and less income. Some relatively simple changes in the way you run your home office can save you an enormous amount of time, which translates into greater success.

Many home office professionals value their freedom to work odd hours, particularly at night or on weekends, when interruptions are few. If you don't get as much done during the day as you'd hoped, you can always get in a few hours in the evening. For some people, the problem is knowing when to stop!

WORKING ALONE

Advantage: No need to worry about office politics or irritating co-workers.

Challenge: Feeling isolated, "out of the loop," and even lonely.

If you have a social nature, be sure to find or create opportunities for face-to-face conversation or you may end up resenting your work and looking for ways to get away from your home office.

When one of my clients, Bev, started a special event company, she was excited about her new business. However, as the months passed she became less and less motivated. Bev missed talking with friends and co-workers in person, and she wasn't enjoying her new lifestyle as much as she thought she would. I suggested that Bev start a local support network made up of other entrepreneurs and home office professionals. She did—and now they meet every two weeks to socialize and share ideas.

SEEING CLIENTS AT HOME

Advantage: You don't waste time traveling to clients or waiting for them to show up.

Challenge: Clients see how you live and work.

Depending upon how tidy you are and where your workspace is located, having clients come to your home can be stressful and possibly embarrassing. If your home office is in, say, a separate wing of the house with a separate entrance, you don't have to worry about clients seeing your laundry or your family's mess. If your office is in a living area of your home, however, you need to think about ways to avoid the need for last-minute cleaning sessions before clients show up. You may find it helpful to use a folding screen, or French doors with curtained panels, or other devices that set your office apart from the rest of the house, draw attention to your workspace, and hide the rest of your home from view.

In a corporate environment, there are a lot of desks, and none are particularly interesting. In a home office, your desk is the center of attention, and it says something about you. Getting and keeping it organized will help you make a professional impression when clients come to your home.

NO DRESS CODE

Advantage: You can work in sweatpants if you feel like it.

Challenge: You have to try harder to achieve a professional appearance when necessary.

I know a graphics designer who works at home who actually puts on a business suit and high heels before making her business calls. This helps her feel professional while she's tackling a difficult call. After she's off the phone, however, she's happy to kick off those heels and get back to work!

As "dressing for success" shows, clothes are more than just pieces of material you happen to have on your body. A professional appearance can help you feel more capable, just as casual clothes can, at times, make you feel at a disadvantage—even if no one is looking at you.

Some people are more sensitive to this issue than others, depending upon their line of work and other factors. My usual advice to clients is to keep all aspects of working at home, from your filing to your attire, as professional as possible.

NO COMMUTING

Advantage: You save time, energy, and money.

Challenge: You can't escape your work.

For convenience, walking twenty steps to your office can't be beat. Whenever I'm stuck in traffic I realize how glad I am that I work at home and generally can avoid being trapped in an unmoving car. On the other hand, when you work at home your job is always present, physically and psychologically.

If you can close the door on your home office, you're lucky. Some home office professionals who don't have a spare room to use as an office design workspaces that close up when not in use. This way their job is less intrusive when they are entertaining or spending time with their family.

MERGING YOUR PERSONAL AND PROFESSIONAL LIVES

Advantage: You can take time during the day for personal calls, errands, and other tasks.

Challenge: Trying to juggle both personal and professional obligations at the same time.

When you work in a corporate office, it's understood that you leave your personal life behind as much as possible. When you work at home, however, there is no escaping your personal life, whether it's last night's dishes, phone calls, bills, the dog, the kids, or all of these. To keep from becoming overwhelmed by personal obligations, try the following:

- Set up your home office in a quiet part of the house, where you won't be interrupted. If at all possible, claim a spare room.

- Install a separate phone line for your business, and put an answering machine on both lines.
- Ignore any personal tasks that aren't essential. Otherwise, you could easily spend all day housecleaning instead of working!
- Put off any personal tasks you can accomplish after hours, such as picking up dry cleaning, buying groceries, or making personal calls.
- Put the remaining essential personal tasks on your "to do" list along with your business obligations, under separate headings.

One of the unique challenges of a home office is that you need to be able to accommodate both your personal and professional records. Although one of my home-based clients has a separate "bill-paying desk," most home office professionals need to find ways to combine the storage of their work files and their home files, such as insurance policies, investment information, tax returns, and product information.

QUICK TIP FOR HOME OFFICE PROFESSIONALS

Don't try to keep your personal and professional lives completely separate. Home office professionals need to find ways to combine their work obligations with their personal tasks in a way that sacrifices neither. It might surprise you to hear that the key to doing this successfully is *not* to try to completely separate your personal and professional lives. I've found that this is not only futile, but inefficient. As you plan your day or your week, write down any personal tasks you need to accomplish, but list them separately from your business tasks. This way you can focus on work-related tasks without losing track of personal obligations.

Several of my home office clients, including both moms and dads, work at home so that one parent can be near the children while the other parent goes off to a corporate office. Paul and Leah feel strongly that one of them should be around for the children, so when Paul was laid off from his corporate job, Leah went back to work and Paul set up a consulting business at home. Although a babysitter comes to the house every day, Paul still finds that he gets interrupted by the kids, as well as called upon to deal with unexpected events. When these situations are important—for example, when their daughter Zoe needed stitches—Paul is particularly glad that he's immediately available. However, interruptions over trivial matters take up his time unnecessarily, break his concentration, make him appear unprofessional, and just plain make him mad.

Paul found that reading the riot act to the children and their sitter was minimally effective, so he called me for ideas. First, we moved his office into the basement. Although Paul initially didn't like the idea of being moved to the "dungeon," he discovered that the benefits of being out of sight, behind a closed door, outweighed the disadvantages of working below ground. Next we set up a two-way intercom system so that Paul could stay in touch with his family without having to leave his office for every small question. We also reserved a drawer in his desk for toys that are brought out only in desperate circumstances, such as when he has to make a business call with a child on his lap. Paul still finds it challenging to work with children in the house, but he also deeply values the close relationship he now has with his kids.

LETTING PEOPLE KNOW YOU MEAN BUSINESS

One of my clients who works at home takes time off every afternoon for a bike ride. He finds this energizes him and clears his mind for another four hours of work. After he missed his bike ride for a week, a neighbor stopped him on the street and asked, "Say, did you find a job?"

Many people believe that if you work at home, you don't have a "real" job and you can't be serious about what you do. Some corporate employees are suspicious of work that doesn't originate in an office building. Obviously these people are missing the point, but their attitude presents a problem for you. To overcome these types of preconceived ideas, people who work at home have to try extra hard to be professional. With that in mind, I recommend that you do the following:

- Maintain normal business hours as much as possible.
- Keep your office businesslike, especially if clients will be seeing it.
- Avoid talking to clients at times when you might be interrupted, particularly by dogs or children.
- Spend the necessary money on quality letterhead stationery.
- Consider using a post office box or mail services box for business mail.

- Be *extra* prompt, *extra* well prepared, and *extra* well groomed when you need to be.
- Project confidence.

If you believe in yourself, others will believe in you, too.

2

■ ■ ■

FINDING
THE RIGHT PLACE
FOR YOUR
HOME OFFICE

It's important to carefully evaluate every room in your home before deciding where your office should be. Even if you have already set up a home office, this is still a useful exercise. There may be a better place for it. Answering the following questions about each space you might use will help you find the ideal location for your home office:

- Will you actually work in this area?
- Will distractions be kept to a minimum?
- Is there (or could there be) ample lighting?
- How difficult would it be to run a phone line into this space?
- Are there enough electrical outlets?
- Is this space comfortable year-round?
- Is there room for everything you need (desk, file cabinet, computer, and so on)?
- Is there room for you to display samples of your work (if needed)?
- Is there enough storage space? Or is there room for storage nearby?

If clients will be coming to your home, also consider the following:

- Can you meet with clients comfortably in this space?
- Is there a separate entrance for clients to use?
- Is there a way to keep clients from seeing the rest of your home?

The only part of your home that clients should see is your office. If possible, have clients use a separate entrance, or locate your office near an entrance. Even though your office may be organized and your presentation professional, you send an entirely different message if you take your clients on a tour through a home that is disorganized.

Unless you do everything yourself, remodeling is expensive. You may have to spend some money fixing up the right spot for your office. For example, you might want phone lines installed or have an electrician put in good lighting or electric heat. Try to think long term. It's better to invest in the right location now than to settle for a space that costs less but will no longer suit your needs in a year or two. If there is any way to avoid it, you don't want to go through the aggravation of moving your office later.

An extra room is the ideal place for a home office, but not everyone has the space. If you don't have a room to spare, the next best choice is to use a portion of an out-of-the-way room such as a guest bedroom or your bedroom. You can also set up a home office within your living room, dining room, family room, or kitchen. Some people successfully convert their basement, garage, or even a closet into a functional workspace. I've seen people make amazing transformations, turning awkward and inconvenient spaces into organized, efficient, comfortable offices.

SOME SPACE-SAVING TRICKS

As you consider your options, keep in mind that you don't necessarily need to set up a traditional office with a big, executive-style desk and an old-fashioned, four-drawer filing cabinet. These days there are many innovative products on the market, some geared specifically to home office professionals, that allow you to be more flexible in your choices.

If you need to keep your workspace compact and unobtrusive, consider installing a drop-leaf, wall-mounted desk to save room. Modular wall systems usually close up when not in use. Another alternative is a desk that

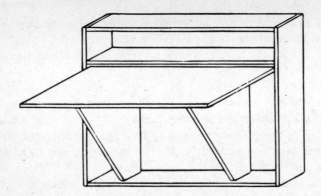

A drop-leaf desk provides workspace during the day but closes up completely when not in use. (Courtesy of Trendlines)

opens up for working but closes into a cabinet when you're finished. A foldup desk like this lets you put your office in any room of your home. A roll-top desk fits in nicely with almost any decor and is useful for hiding papers or work in progress.

If you plan to set up your home office in a living area—for example, in your living room, dining room, or guest room—consider using a rolling computer cart and a rolling file cart. Even a large desk can be put on coasters. When you entertain, all you have to do is push your office furniture against the wall or into another room.

SAMPLE LAYOUTS

Included in the following pages are some sample layouts showing how you might meet the challenge of finding a place at home for your office. Each layout includes the following basic home office essentials:

- Desk
- Chair
- Fax
- Personal computer (PC)
- Printer
- Shelves
- Filing cabinet

Exactly how you lay out your office depends on many factors, including the size and shape of the space that's available and the type of furniture and equipment you choose. As you read this book, you'll make many decisions that will affect your workspace. You'll also find the right location for many smaller items—for example, your phone, answering machine, and various office organizing products—that aren't pictured here. These layouts are intended to help you think about the various options your home provides.

THE SPARE ROOM

Advantage: The perfect solution, if you have the space.

Disadvantage: None.

Having an entire room to devote to your office is the ideal situation. You have plenty of space in which to consolidate everything related to your job, you can work in privacy, distractions are minimized, you don't have to worry about putting all of your papers away when guests come over, and at the end of the day you can close the door behind you and enjoy the rest of your home. Also, a separate office is the most professional place in which to meet clients.

Before you cross this option off your list, consider whether or not you have a seldom-used room—for example, a dining room—that could be converted into an office. Attic or loft spaces are other possibilities to think about.

If you have the luxury of converting a spare room into an office, do an absolutely thorough job of it. Take the seasonal clothing out of the closet and remove any hobby equipment you're storing there. Limit everything in the room to work-related items, and use this room only for working.

THE GUEST BEDROOM

Advantage: Almost as good as setting up your office in a spare room.

Disadvantage: Inconvenient when guests actually visit.

In that it is extremely helpful to have your office in a separate, out-of-the-way room that has a door, rearranging a guest bedroom so that it can accommodate your home office is definitely better than having your office in a portion of a room with more traffic, such as a family room.

In order to have your guest room double as your office (or is it vice versa?), you may have to invest in a hideaway bed. Another alternative is a Murphy bed. Murphy beds are making a comeback, but today, instead of being built into the wall, they come in cabinets so that if you move you can take your Murphy bed with you.

If you need to keep your guest bedroom relatively intact—for example, maybe you have regular visitors who need access to a bed, a dresser, and some shelves—designate a corner of the room as your office. You might reserve a drawer or two of the dresser for office supplies. One of my clients used folding screens to surround her work area. When she stepped behind them and sat at her desk, she was ready to work—and her guests didn't feel they were intruding on her private workspace.

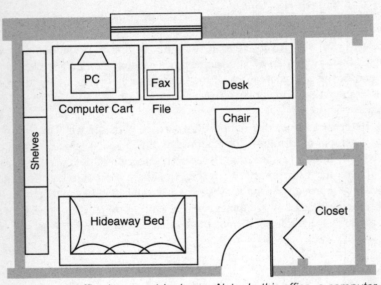

How to set up an office in a guest bedroom. Note: In this office, a computer cart holds both a computer (on top) and a printer (underneath). With this arrangement, you would need blinds or curtains in the window to cut down on glare.

YOUR BEDROOM

Advantage: It's good to have your office in a separate room, even if it has to be your bedroom.

Disadvantage: Sleeping with your work.

I usually advise clients not to put their home office in their bedroom if there is any way to avoid it. However, if you have to choose between setting up your office in your bedroom or in a portion of another living area in your

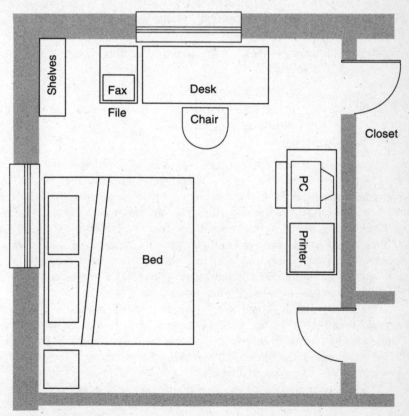

How to set up an office in your bedroom.

home in which you will have absolutely no privacy, choose the bedroom. The advantages of working in a separate room without constant interruptions outweigh the inconveniences of sleeping with your job. With a little ingenuity, you can design a workspace that closes up or is hidden from view after hours, allowing you to sleep in peace.

When your office is in your bedroom, you'll probably have only limited storage space, so you'll need to think about other areas in which to store your work-related materials. If clients will be coming to your home, you'll probably want to clean up the dining room and meet with them there.

THE LIVING ROOM, DINING ROOM, OR FAMILY ROOM

Advantage: You have plenty of room in which to spread out your papers while you work.

Disadvantage: In a living area, it's difficult to keep your personal life from intruding on your work.

When your office is in a corner of a living area of your home, there is constant friction between your work life and your personal life. If you live quietly by yourself, or if the area you choose is seldom used, the inconveniences are certainly manageable (for example, having to clean up before entertaining). However, if you live with others, you can expect their need to use this shared living space to conflict with your needs. You may be interrupted often, your paperwork is at risk when others have access to your desk, and it's more difficult to concentrate when you're surrounded by other people's clutter (not to mention your own).

One of my clients turned his living room into a studio very successfully. He found it served his needs *better* than the spare room he had been using. However, for the most part he had this territory to himself. During the day he was alone in the house, and his wife seldom ventured into the living room unless they were entertaining.

If you live in a one-bedroom apartment and can't set up your office in your bedroom, you have to create a workspace in the living area of your apartment. You may have to sacrifice having a separate dining area. Use high shelves to separate your workspace from the rest of your apartment.

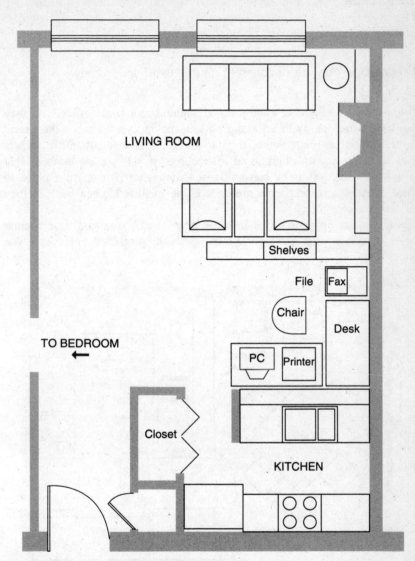

LIVING ROOM

Shelves

File   Fax

Chair

Desk

TO BEDROOM ←

PC   Printer

Closet

KITCHEN

How to set up an office in your living room.

THE KITCHEN

Advantage: You can stay in contact with your family.

Disadvantage: You are in constant contact with your family.

If you have a kitchen big enough to accommodate a home office, you may also have a big family to go along with it, making your kitchen the Grand Central Station of your home. If your kitchen sees a lot of traffic, expect constant interruptions, clutter, and distractions. If you use the kitchen table as a work area, you'll be constantly shuffling your papers from place to place. However, some people prefer working in their kitchen because they feel comfortable there.

   If you set up your office in the kitchen, make sure you have a clear area in which to work and a place to put your filing cabinet. You could even

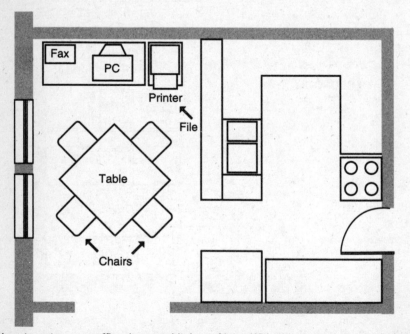

How to set up an office in your kitchen. Note: With this arrangement, shelves could be mounted on the wall above the desk.

put a tablecloth over it when you're not working so that it blends in with its surroundings.

THE BASEMENT

Advantage: An out-of-the-way place in which to work.

Disadvantage: Can be depressing: dark, damp, and/or lonely.

A basement office has all of the advantages of an office in a separate room, including privacy, few distractions, and a single area in which to put all of your work-related items. If you can transform your basement (or, more likely, a portion of your basement) into a brightly lit, comfortable work area, this is a good option for you. On the other hand, if you like to be near windows while you work, or if your basement is damp, musty, or smells of furnace fumes, look elsewhere.

Brenda, a district manager for a line of cosmetics, called me because she was struggling daily to find enough time to fill orders, call her sales reps, and meet with clients. When I went to Brenda's home to consult with her, it was obvious that her biggest problem was the lack of a regular place in which to work. Some days she worked in her bedroom; other days she used the kitchen table.

We developed a plan for turning Brenda's basement into a home office. She had the walls covered with sheetrock and painted white; then she added carpeting, track lighting, and built-in shelves. Her new office has changed the way she works, as well as the way she feels about her work.

THE GARAGE

Advantage: Working in an area separated from the rest of your home, and thus more private.

Disadvantage: Losing the use of your garage for other purposes.

By remodeling your garage into a home office, you can create a quiet, private workspace that is completely set off from the rest of the house. The downside of creating a garage office is that the remodeling can be expensive and you may miss being able to use that space for parking your car and storing your lawn mower. Depending how big your garage is, you might remodel part of it and share it with your car.

A garage is a good alternative for you if you want to work at home but still want the feeling of "going to the office" each day. One of my clients, a bookkeeper, liked the freedom of working at home, yet wanted to keep her office and her home separate. She used to have her office in a spare bedroom, but she found she couldn't walk past the door without going in and doing some work.

To satisfy her needs, she converted her garage into an office. She added insulation and a window so that she could use a window air-conditioning unit in the summer and a space heater in the winter. When she went to work she would leave through the front door of her house and enter her office through a side door in her garage. By physically separating her office from her home, she was able to have the feeling of working outside her home without having to commute.

CLOSETS

Advantage: A compact office behind closed doors.

Disadvantages: Limited space, and the loss of the use of your closet for storage.

A large closet can be converted into a nice little work area. You'll need to install some overhead shelves for storage, a flat surface for your desktop, and a file cabinet next to (or under) your work surface. If your closet has sliding doors, you'll need to change them into regular doors so that both can be open while you work. Another option is to fully open up the length of the closet and install folding accordion-style doors. To hide everything from view after hours, choose a chair that fits under your desktop.

CLEARING OUT YOUR CHOSEN OFFICE SPACE

Now that you've decided where you are going to set up your office, you have to go through your office-to-be and remove the things that don't belong there. Many people find it easier to store something than to make the

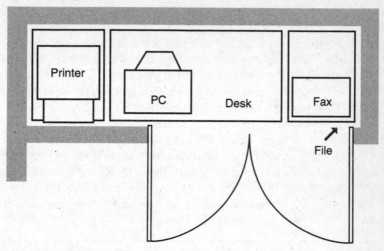

How to set up a closet office. Note: This arrangement requires a closet space at least three feet deep and nine feet long. The chair could be stored either under the desk or outside the closet when not in use. Shelves could be placed above the desk.

decision to keep it or to throw it away. Use this opportunity to move items you no longer need right out of the house, rather than rearrange junk.

Getting rid of possessions can be difficult. Some people feel they are throwing away a part of themselves or their history when they get rid of something. Others hate to get rid of something that is in perfectly good shape or that seems as if it might be useful someday.

The biggest problem with being a pack rat is that you accumulate too much clutter. Eventually clutter interferes with your efficiency, not only because you run out of places to store everything, but because you get so absorbed in "making do" with items you already have that you may miss valuable new opportunities. You also end up wasting time and energy resurrecting or wearing out old items when it's actually far simpler and even cheaper to buy exactly what you need when you need it.

When you keep too many things, eventually you lose track of what you have and where everything is. As we're clearing out their desks, clients of mine often say, "I've been looking for that," or, "I didn't even know I had that!" The things you really do need can get buried under the extra items you would be better off without.

You may be afraid that the minute you throw something away, you'll need it. Everyone has experienced this phenomenon. However, what you have to realize is that *before* you got rid of those old ice skates, or your books from college, or the pickle dish your Aunt Ida gave you, chances are you had either forgotten you had it or forgotten where it was. Either way, it actually wasn't of any use to you. When you keep only those things you need, you'll know what you have and where everything is—and the useful items won't get buried under the items you don't need.

James, a researcher, needed help decluttering a spare bedroom before he could use it as a home office. When I walked into the room, there were boxes stacked in the closet and against the wall. He told me he had recently moved in and hadn't had time to unpack them. When I discovered that in fact he'd been living in his home for two years, the decluttering job suddenly got easier. Anything you don't even look at for two years can probably be safely thrown out, donated, or sold.

QUICK TIP FOR HOME OFFICE PROFESSIONALS

The "Toss or Keep?" Test. There are three questions to ask yourself to determine whether or not you should keep something.

1. Have I used this item within the past year?
2. Is it serving a specific purpose?
3. Do I have a place to store it where I can find it again?

If you answered no to any of these questions, consider giving or throwing the item away. If you decide to keep it, make sure you can find it when you need it!

A STEP-BY-STEP PLAN FOR DECLUTTERING

Cleaning out your chosen office space will take time. How long it will take depends on the size of the space, the amount of stuff you have there already, and how long you've been accumulating things in this space. Schedule enough time to work on this project without interruption until it is completed. If you have to stop in the middle, you may not be able to finish for another week. This means you'll spend a week stepping over all of the things you're trying to organize, and you may end up pushing all of the clutter back into your office space again. The following are recommendations for clearing out your chosen space.

1. *Take out any large items (furniture, skis, exercise machines, luggage, and so on) that don't belong in your office and put them elsewhere.* Some people keep a television set in their office for work-related viewing, but most people are better off without one around.

2. *Get four large bags in which to place the remaining smaller items.* The point of using the bags is to keep you focused on your office. If you have to leave to put an item away, you may get sidetracked. Label the bags respectively as follows:

- Give away (charity items)
- Put away (items that belong in other rooms in your home)
- Storage
- Trash

3. *Work systematically.* Start by decluttering one corner of your office area and work your way around the room. It's important to focus on just one section at a time. I've found that a clockwise approach works best and reduces the tendency to jump from section to section.

4. *Go back to the large items.* Use the system you used for the smaller items: give them away, put them elsewhere in your home, put them in storage, or throw them out.

This is a big decluttering project, but if it's done correctly, you should never have to do it again, especially to this degree. Although things will look terrible when your office space is in transition, don't get discouraged. The end result will be well worth the time you spend.

QUICK TIP FOR HOME OFFICE PROFESSIONALS

When you're cleaning up, try to decide quickly what to do with each item. Don't put off making up your mind, because delaying doesn't make the process any easier. Avoid making a "decide later" pile. As you begin to get tired, everything will end up in that pile—and nothing will get thrown out!

STAYING DECLUTTERED

To keep your office decluttered in the future, I recommend the following:

- Don't bring anything into your work area without first asking yourself if you really need it.
- Keep only work-related items in your office.
- Whenever an item breaks, whether it's a pen or a printer, either get it fixed within a week or get rid of it.

One of the best ways to keep your office uncluttered is to set up organizing systems that help you process your paperwork efficiently. In the next chapter, we'll start with a basic: how to arrange your workspace.

3 ▧ ▧ ▧

ARRANGING
YOUR WORKSPACE

Your home office can be as basic or as elaborate as you want, but the way it is laid out will affect your productivity. The key is to make it work for you. It has to be a place you enjoy, and it has to be organized in a way that both suits your working style and meets your business needs efficiently.

ORGANIZING FROM THE GROUND UP

Organizing your workspace to suit your needs is the first step to taking control of your home office. Once you start thinking in terms of greater efficiency, you are on your way to organizing every aspect of your business.

People have told me that they were born disorganized and will probably die disorganized. You don't have to be born organized in order to get organized. Getting organized requires what I call the four keys to organization: acknowledgment, desire, direction, and action.

1. *Acknowledgment.* First you have to admit that your home office needs to be organized. Even if in reality your office already works for you, you

probably could make changes that would contribute to your greater productivity.

2. *Desire.* You won't alter your habits or your habitat unless you see a need and want to change. A motivating idea that works for most people is the fact that organizing is the key to greater professional success.

3. *Direction.* Once you've acknowledged a need to change, professional advice is helpful in getting you started. Although organizing your home office is largely a matter of common sense, there are tricks, products, and systems of which you may be unaware. This book will give you the direction you need to implement changes.

4. *Action.* Good intentions alone won't get you organized. Now that you've located the best place for your home office, it's time to take action.

WHERE TO BEGIN

Here's a game plan for setting up your own personalized workspace. Developing exactly the right layout for you will take time, so please don't try to rush through these steps. The more thought you put into your office layout up front, the fewer adjustments you'll need to make later.

1. *Write down your needs.* Do you need an office that will comfortably accommodate clients? Do you need space for samples, or forms, or reference books? Do you need special shelves or flat files for watercolor paper or architectural renderings? Do you need to fit in a drafting table or a large, open surface for cutting fabric or laying out paperwork? How would you arrange your ideal office and what would you put in it?

2. *Consider your options.* In this chapter you'll find three basic sample layouts to think about. Most offices roughly follow one of these arrangements, but the possibilities are endless. What are the advantages and limitations of your chosen space?

3. *Think about furniture.* What do you have on hand, and what do you need to buy? Maybe you can raid a table or desk or chair from another part of the house. (Warning: if existing furniture doesn't quite suit your needs, don't try to make do with it. It will only cause you irritation.) Furniture manufacturers are finally realizing the need for affordable, good quality furniture for home offices and are now making it available.

4. *Read the rest of this book for ideas.* You may find that there's a product you weren't aware of, or a way of handling paperwork that requires a certain type of file cabinet, or a way to use your wall space to your advantage. Before you make up your mind about how you want to arrange your workspace, review the organizational methods that will best work for you.

5. *Plan your office on a grid.* It's a good idea to measure your office space, draw it on a grid, and then fit in any furniture you plan to use. To make the best use of your space, you may discover that you need to go out and buy a desk or table that is exactly 40 inches long—not 38, and not 42. Playing around with various arrangements on a paper grid beats wrestling with actual furniture, and you can think more clearly when you aren't surrounded by office equipment.

6. *Shop for what you need.* Bring your grid as well as a list of what you need to buy, with exact dimensions. The fewer surprises you have at the end of this process, the better.

Like dessert, the best part comes last. After you've been through all of these steps, you'll be ready to move in.

QUICK TIP FOR HOME OFFICE PROFESSIONALS

It's never too late to change. If you want to get organized, you can. If you want to improve, you can. People have different reasons—personal, professional, psychological—for wanting to get organized. Some people realize they are overwhelmed and want to reduce their stress level. Others are ashamed of themselves for being disorganized. Many people would like to have more free time, and everyone would like to have more money. Keep your personal motivation in mind as you implement new organizational strategies.

CHOOSING A BASIC LAYOUT

Take a look at the three basic layouts that follow and see which appeals to you and might work in your available space. Keep in mind that this is only a first step. In later chapters you'll be refining your workspace so that it is fully customized to suit your needs. The following layouts include the same office essentials as the layouts in Chapter 2:

- Desk
- Chair
- Fax
- Personal computer (PC)

- Printer
- Shelves
- Filing cabinet

If you have other sizable office equipment—for example, a copier, drafting table, flat file, or floor lamp—start thinking about how they might fit into your overall design.

■ The U-Shaped Work Area

If your office has additional workspace to both the left and right of your desk, you have a U-shaped work area. For example, to the left of your desk you might have a computer cart, and to the right you might have a table with a fax machine and a phone/answering machine. This layout is extremely convenient. All you have to do is swivel your chair one way or the other while you work. Possible disadvantages are that it requires a lot of space and in some cases you may have to face your desk to the wall (not optimal for seeing clients).

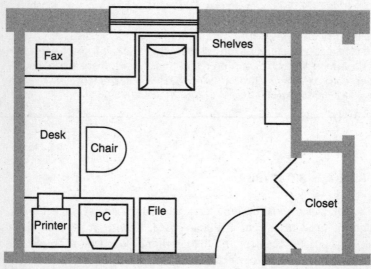

The U-shaped work area.

■ The L-Shaped Work Area

The L-shaped work area takes up less space than the U-shaped work area but still offers the important advantage of getting equipment off your desk and onto a secondary surface. For example, on a table next to your desk you could place your computer, typewriter, or phone, leaving your desk clear for work in progress.

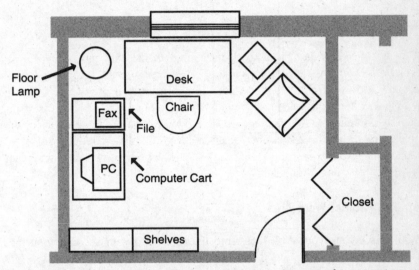

The L-shaped work area. Note: This arrangement makes use of a computer cart that stores the computer on top and the printer underneath.

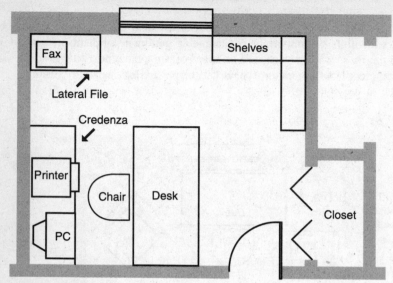

The parallel work area.

■ The Parallel Work Area

With this layout, your desk faces into the room and your secondary surface is behind you.

REFINING YOUR MASTER PLAN

As you think about how to arrange your workspace, keep in mind the following general office-organizing guidelines:

- *Keep related items near one another.* For example, arrange your computer and printer so they are next to each other, and put your computer reference books on a shelf above them. Store all of your paper—printer paper, fax paper, legal pads (whatever you use)—in the same place.
- *Keep the items you use often close at hand.* The things you

need constantly should be within reach. Items you use occasionally should go in drawers or in a closet in your home office. Work-related items you seldom use or files you rarely refer to should be boxed up and stored. As a last resort, store this seldom-used information in another room. Store it together, and limit it to one other room. When you start stashing it around your home, you'll forget that you own it. Finally, items you never use should be gotten rid of.

■ *You'll need some files in or next to your desk.* These help keep papers off your desk but within easy reach (see Chapter 5 for ideas).

CHOOSING OFFICE FURNITURE

The following are some helpful tips for choosing the major pieces of furniture that will be going into your home office. Use these guidelines to avoid making a home office professional's most common mistakes.

■ Desks

■ If you like to squirrel things away, *don't* buy a desk with drawers. You'll just end up stuffing things in them.

■ If you're not a pack rat, buy a desk that has enough drawer space to hold your everyday items. This will help keep your desktop clear. A desk file drawer is also helpful for keeping papers you are currently working on nearby but out of sight. Don't buy a desk that has so much extra room that you'll end up stuffing it full of unnecessary items.

■ A big desk doesn't make you organized, and a small desk doesn't make you efficient. However, a big desk gives you a lot of room to spread out papers when you need to.

■ Choose a desk that's the right height so that you won't be hunched over while you work.

■ If you have carpeting under your desk, get a plastic mat to put under your chair. It makes getting around easier and reduces wear and tear on your carpet.

Gene, a retired accountant, purchased the desk he had used for twenty years in his corporate job and brought it to his home office. After a few months, he started to regret ever having bought it. It had served him well in his corporate job, but it was too large for his home office. Also, it had no file drawer—something he needed now that he no longer had access to the large filing cabinets he'd had at work. Gene ended up selling his old desk and buying a smaller desk with file space.

■ Filing Cabinets

Depending on your filing needs and budget, you may want to consider options other than the traditional two- or four-drawer filing cabinet. There are various factors you need to keep in mind.

- How much money do you want to spend?
- How much room do you have in your office?
- How much paperwork do you have?
- What future filing needs do you anticipate?

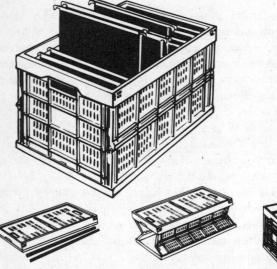

A collapsible filing crate folds flat, unfolds quickly, and is useful for temporary filing needs. (Courtesy of Cadence, Inc.)

The following are some file storage options:

The traditional two- or four-drawer vertical filing cabinet. If you choose one of these, make sure you get a sturdy one. What may seem to be a bargain on a low-quality cabinet may cost you more in the long run when you have to struggle to open and close the drawers, if the drawer falls on your foot, if you have to replace the handles, or if the entire thing gives out. Some file cabinets are deeper than others, so keep your office space in mind as you shop.

Lateral filing cabinets hold your folders sideways instead of front to back. They take up more space horizontally, but have less depth. One of the nice benefits of a lateral file is that it provides a secondary work surface on top.

Open-front files are specialized files most commonly seen in medical offices, where there is constant retrieval and refiling of individual files. They do not accommodate hanging folders, and require special file folders that allow you to easily read the label on each folder.

Open file carts are most often used for work in progress (see page 60). However, if you have a limited amount of space in your office and a limited number of files, a file cart would work for you. One disadvantage of the open file cart is that its contents are visible to anyone who walks into your office.

File crates with file rods inside will hold a large number of hanging folders. They come in both rigid and collapsible types.

Open file crates, similar to milk crates, can be used either on a flat surface, open at the top, or stacked vertically, laid on their sides. If you use a file crate open at the top, you insert hanging folders so that they hook over the edges of the crate. If you use the crates with the open side facing out, you would use accordion files or file jackets (see page 118) to hold your papers. One of my clients, the owner of a home-based talent agency, used wire stacking crates with expanding folders to hold all of the video and audio tapes she constantly received.

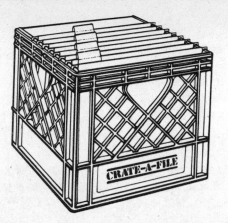

"Milk crate" filing crates hold hanging folders and fit in just about anywhere.
(Courtesy of W.T. Rogers)

Cardboard file boxes with lids are appropriate for files you need to store away somewhere but seldom refer to.

If you have extremely valuable papers you wish to file at home, consider investing in a fireproof file box or filing cabinet. If you're a pack rat, don't go overboard with file cabinets. You'll only find a way to fill them up.

■ Combination Machines

You can save space by buying a machine that does more than one job—for example, a fax-copier, or a phone/answering machine. Check the quality of these machines carefully. In some cases, you will be sacrificing the capability of one feature in order to include another.

QUICK TIP FOR HOME OFFICE PROFESSIONALS

When space is at a premium, use vertical space. For example, a computer cart stores your computer and printer vertically, leaving you with more surface area on which to work.

Cardboard file boxes, especially useful for storage, are affordable on any budget. (Courtesy of Perma Products Company)

CHEAP TRICKS

Creating an efficient home office doesn't have to cost a fortune. The following tips are for you if you're interested in saving money:

- Instead of buying a bona fide desk, put a board or door across the top of two filing cabinets. You could also use a kitchen table or an antique dressing table with the mirror removed. (Warning: if a smooth writing surface is important to you, a newer surface is probably better. Or, get a blotter.)
- Instead of buying new bookshelves, convert a closet into shelves. You can also add a light and turn this into a display area for samples of your work.
- Add storage space in your closet for small office supplies by hanging a clear plastic shoe holder.

ARRANGING YOUR OFFICE FURNITURE

Keep the following pointers in mind as you lay out your office:

- In a home office, it's not necessary to make your desk face out or face the door unless clients come to your home. I have mine against the wall because it makes my office feel more open.
- If possible, don't put your computer in front of a window. The glare will be hard on your eyes. Make sure your computer screen is either facing a wall without a window or at a right angle to a window, instead of in front of it, for better viewing. If you have to place your computer before a window, make sure you have curtains or blinds to block the outside light while you're looking at your monitor.
- Don't put your fax machine in a location where incoming documents might get lost. I have one client who was unaware that fax transmissions were piling up behind her filing cabinet!
- Don't forget to allow space for opening filing cabinet drawers—about an additional twenty-four inches for a vertical filing cabinet or one foot for a lateral filing cabinet. The cabinet itself may fit in a convenient space next to your shelves, but it's useless if you can't open the drawers all the way.
- If you have a hideaway bed in your office, make sure you leave enough room in front of it to open and close it easily, especially if you use it often. This way you'll cause less disruption to your office when you need to use the bed.

QUICK TIP FOR HOME OFFICE PROFESSIONALS

Don't try to organize everything in one day. It took awhile to get to the level of disorganization you now encounter. If you try to do everything at once, there's a high risk of getting discouraged and giving up altogether. Break the job down into manageable chunks and tackle one thing at a time. Make a list of everything you'd like to accomplish, and reward yourself for each task completed. Scheduling several interruption-free afternoons is usually a more successful approach than trying to organize your entire business life in a day.

USING A PLANNING GRID

To use a planning grid, you'll need to make or buy graph paper with half-inch squares. On the grid, each one-half inch square corresponds to one foot of office space. You can use a finer grid if you wish, but probably half-inch squares are adequate.

Begin by drawing a rough aerial (bird's-eye view) of your office space on a piece of blank paper. Be sure to include any permanent fixtures, such as windows, doors, and radiators. Then measure your office space exactly and draw a more precise layout on grid paper.

After your space is mapped out on the grid, you might want to run some copies of it for doodling on. When you're ready to get serious, create to-scale cutouts of your office furniture and move them around on your grid. You'll need symbols for office items such as the following:

- Computer (typewriter, word processor)
- Copier
- Desk and chair
- Drafting table
- Fax
- Filing cabinet
- Floor lamp
- Printer
- Telephone/answering machine

To make the best possible use of your walls (see Chapter 5), you might consider drawing floor-to-ceiling elevated views of your wall space. First, draw anything permanent, such as wall switches or windows; then add the following:

- Bulletin board
- Shelves
- Wall clock

Some people avoid working with a planning grid because they can't draw. You really don't have to be able to draw to be able to push cutouts around on a piece of paper. Planning your office on paper is a valuable exercise because you may come up with some unexpected results that wouldn't have occurred to you if you were standing in the middle of your chosen space.

You may find that you want to add some stacking bins to your office, or a rolling file cart, or some milk crates for storage. Before deciding on a final floor plan (and wall plan) for your office, I urge you to read on.

4

BUYING
AND STORING
OFFICE SUPPLIES

Office supplies are all of those small but essential items that enable you to work. Without pens and paper and files and envelopes, your home office would be useless.

The people who own the Staples chain of office supply stores figured this out awhile ago. Their radio ad caught my attention.

> To succeed in business, you don't need to be big. All you need is a dream. Just a dream and the passion to pursue it. And the dedication to see it through. The talent to build it on. And the opportunity to use your talent. And a little luck. And some pencils. And pens. Maybe some typewriter ribbons and correction fluid. And some of those little yellow note pads with the sticky stuff on the back. And some of those envelopes with the little windows in them so you can send out bills. And you can save a bundle on all of these things at Staples, the office superstore.*

*Radio ad by Jay Williams; Hill Holliday, Connors, Cosmopulos, Inc., Advertising, Boston.

Office supplies matter because they make a difference in how effective you are.

1. *You can't work without them.* If you've ever run out of ink for your printer in the middle of a job, you've experienced firsthand how one missing item can cause your entire workday to grind to a halt.

2. *Some products are specifically designed to keep you organized.* Many office products are designed for the sole purpose of helping you handle your paperwork and manage your time more efficiently, which translates into greater productivity.

3. *The right tools help you work faster.* A paper folder and stamp moistener help you get out a mailing quickly; a postal scale helps cut down on trips to the post office; even a staple remover saves you time.

4. *Some items help you look professional.* Printed stationery, for example, presents a polished image, which is especially important for a home office professional.

As a home-based professional, you need to be aware of the full range of office supplies available to you and how you can use them to best advantage. Moreover, in that you don't have a corporate supply closet to raid when you run out of something, you need to set up a system that not only allows you to store an adequate supply of office products but lets you see at a glance when you're running low.

Chapter 3 discussed the larger items that belong in your home office, such as a desk, filing cabinet, and electronic equipment. Now use the following lists to see how well equipped you are with the smaller items.

BASIC HOME OFFICE SUPPLIES
ONE-TIME PURCHASES

Business card holder (either card file or notebook)

Calculator

Check endorsement stamp

Clear shoeboxes to hold office supplies

Computer disk holders

Daily planner (or desk calendar or pocket calendar)

Date stamp

Drawer dividers (or trays)

Electric pencil sharpener

Hanging file frames for filing cabinet

BASIC HOME OFFICE SUPPLIES (continued)

Letter opener
Paper cutter
Petty cash box
Postal scale (may be leased)
Ruler
Scissors
Stamp holder
Stamp moistener

Stapler
Staple remover
Surge protector
Tape dispenser
Three-hole punch
Three-ring binders
Vertical file holder
Wastebasket

BASIC HOME OFFICE SUPPLIES
ITEMS YOU'LL NEED TO REPLENISH

Address labels
Adhesive note pads
Business cards (yours, imprinted)
Cellophane tape
Clear labels
Computer disks
Computer paper
Copy paper (white, 20-lb., 8½"
    by 11")
Correction fluid (white, plus color
    to match letterhead)
Correction tape (used to cover
    mistakes)
Erasers
Fax paper
Hanging file folders (plus clear
    plastic tabs and inserts)
Highlighter markers
Interior file folders
Labels for file folders
Laser-printer paper

Legal pads
Mailing labels
Manila envelopes (9" × 12" and
    10" × 13")
Note-size stationery (imprinted
    paper and envelopes)
Overnight-delivery packing sup-
    plies (envelopes and labels)
Paper clips
Pencils
Pens
Petty cash receipt book
Printer ink (ribbons or cartridges)
Rubber bands
Stamps
Staples
Stationery (imprinted letterhead,
    plain second sheets, im-
    printed envelopes)
Typewriter supplies (ribbons, cor-
    rection tapes)

Add to this list any supplies that are specific to your business. Then copy the list and refer to it whenever you're stocking up on office supplies.

You could even keep a copy near your supply closet, circling the items you need to buy on your next trip to the store.

QUICK TIP FOR HOME OFFICE PROFESSIONALS

Buy an extra set of office supplies for your family to use. Keep them stored in an area outside your office so that no one will raid your supplies.

FINDING THE RIGHT PRODUCTS FOR YOU

There are unused office products stashed in closets throughout the country. Do *not* buy anything that is just going to clutter up your workspace, no matter how appealing it seems.

Dave, a home-based psychologist, confessed to me after one of my seminars that he kept buying office organizing products, thinking each new item would solve his problem with being disorganized. Instead, this created a new problem: lack of space in which to put all of the products he had bought!

I know many people periodically seized by an urge to get organized. They rush to the local office supply store and buy every product guaranteed to save them time, energy, and irritation. Then, mysteriously, their enthusiasm begins to decrease and their frustration with these products increases. Eventually they slip back into their old habits, convinced they will never be organized and feeling even worse than they did before. Instead of blaming the products, they blame themselves.

Similarly, I've seen people try to mimic their more organized friends by buying the same products and hoping to get the same results. However, the fact that a product works for someone else doesn't mean it will work for you. When it comes to organizing, everyone has different needs, and these needs have to be met differently.

Companies devote endless hours to developing products to fit consumers' needs. They come up with a product, work with focus groups, and refine the product based on the results of these groups. But even all of this effort does not ensure that a product is perfect or will work for you.

Instead of trying to adapt yourself to a product, whether it's a fountain pen or a drawer organizer or a calendar, find a product that suits your needs. To do this, you must first identify the areas in which you're having organizational problems.

I can't tell you what to run out and buy, but I can show you some organizational methods that word for various personality types. After reading the rest of this book, you'll know exactly where you need to focus your energies. You may find that there's a filing system you should implement, or a daily planner that would solve your scheduling troubles. Once you know what you need, go out and find the right product *for you*. Then you *will* use it, it *won't* clutter up your office, and you *will* be organized.

QUICK TIP FOR HOME OFFICE PROFESSIONALS

Don't expect any product to organize you. Many people believe that a helpful product should automatically make them organized. Nothing will organize you. You use products to organize yourself. Believing that an organizational product should get you organized is like expecting your car to drive you somewhere on its own.

KEEPING COSTS DOWN

Large corporations and small businesses alike waste hundreds, even thousands of dollars each year on unnecessary office supplies. A large corporation may not notice these extra dollars right away, but in a small business, every dollar counts. There are several ways you can keep office supply costs down.

1. *Always use a list when you go to the store.* A list keeps you from buying what you don't need and reminds you of what you do need to buy. Most people end up spending a little more than they expected every time they go to the store. By using a list, you'll remember to get everything you need, and you'll save money by making fewer trips to the store.
2. *Buy only what you need, in the quantity you need.* To reduce the amount of time you spend shopping, buy enough office supplies for at least two months. When you first start working in your home office, you won't know exactly how much to buy, but after awhile you'll develop a pattern and you'll know how long supplies will last.
3. *Don't buy more than you can efficiently store.* Buying large quantities of office supplies can be cost effective, but extra supplies won't save you

money if they get ruined in the basement, if you forget you have them, or if you can't find them when you need them. If you can't immediately get your hands on a certain item, you'll probably go out and buy another, so you end up replacing what you've already got. Hint: many supplies are cheaper by the case; consider splitting the cost with another home office professional.

4. *Before you buy anything on sale, make sure you need it.* Someone once told me, "If it's on sale, and you don't need it, it's not a bargain."

5. *Buy from discount office supply stores.* The prices at superstores are usually 40 percent lower than those of traditional office supply stores.

6. *Buy quality.* Both quality and quantity count. Sometimes when you buy something that seems like a bargain, you end up getting what you paid for.

7. *Replenish your supplies before you run out.* Buying ahead of need gives you a chance to comparison shop and take advantage of sales. Also, running out at the last minute for a needed item is an inefficient use of time.

8. *Squeeze all the life you can out of your supplies.* For example, laser-printer cartridges can usually be cleaned out and refilled three times before you need to buy a new cartridge.

STORING EXTRA OFFICE SUPPLIES

When it comes to office supplies, you have two storage needs: a place to put your extra supplies, and places to put the items you use during the day that need to be stored but not hidden away.

If your home office has more than one user, it's vital that you keep all of your supplies—both your extra supplies and the everyday variety—labeled. If more than one person will be looking for the correction fluid, or a blank computer disk, or a fresh ream of copy paper, label where everything goes so that all hands can see at a glance where everything belongs and the office can keep running smoothly. Put labels on the outside of drawers, on shelves, on clear plastic containers—wherever items are placed when they're not in use.

Before fine-tuning your desktop (see Chapter 5), establish a single place in which to store all of your backup supplies. You can use a closet, an empty dresser, stacking bins, or wire shelves—whatever you like that works in your office space. What you want to avoid is stashing small piles of extra supplies in various places around your office.

When you work at home, it's tempting to store extra supplies in other parts of your abode. Bad idea! Resist the urge to stash items away wherever there's room in your home. Instead of looking for additional places to store supplies, cut down on the amount of supplies you already have. Limiting the number of places you have to look for something will limit the amount of time you spend looking. Also, every time you have to leave your office, you run the risk of getting sidetracked in another part of your home.

If you absolutely have to, build shelves for backup supplies in a designated area of your garage or basement. Reserve this area for items you won't be needing for a few months. The following ideas will help you store your supplies efficiently so that you'll never hear yourself say, "I didn't know I had that!"

1. *Store the same type of items together,* so that when you look for something, there's only one place to look. Keep all of your pens, pencils, and markers together, all of your filing supplies together, and all VCR and cassette tapes together. When all related items are stored together, you're never in doubt about where to find something.

2. *Keep supplies, grouped by type, in clear containers.* Label the outsides of the containers and store them next to containers holding related items.

3. *Post a list near your supplies* to help you keep track of what you have and what you need. This list should include everything you need to have on hand (see the chart on page 48).

4. *Take backup items out of their original packaging to save room.* Those clear containers mentioned already are a more efficient use of space.

In the next chapter, we'll take a look at another challenge: how to store the items and papers you use every day so that they are accessible and organized.

QUICK TIP FOR HOME OFFICE PROFESSIONALS

"A place for everything, and everything in its place." Many of us were raised hearing this statement, and it's still valid. It's important to determine, early in your quest for an organized office, where everything will go. If you do this correctly, there will be only *one* place to look for any particular item—and only *one* place to store it when it isn't in use.

5

CLEARING OFF
YOUR DESK

Whether you are setting up a brand new office or organizing an existing one, chances are you have all types of things on your desk. If you're relatively organized already, you might have only some stacks of paperwork, a few pens, some paper clips, some objects you enjoy, and maybe some notes to yourself. If you're not at all organized, you might have old batteries, food, magazines, and who knows what else.

Guess what? *It all has to go.* Not necessarily into the wastebasket, but into files, into drawers, onto shelves, or onto a surface other than your desk. The only papers on your desk should be the ones you are referring to; the only objects should be ones you use often.

A messy desk is *not* the sign of a creative mind, nor, as I often hear, is a clean desk the sign of a sick mind. Some people honestly believe that a clear desk will prevent them from being creative, while others realize that a cluttered desk often leads to a cluttered mind.

If you like to keep your desk buried and find that works for you, nothing I say will convince you to change your ways. However, if the clutter starts to interfere with your productivity, make a few modifications along the guidelines that follow.

WHAT BELONGS ON YOUR DESK

An ideal way to decide what should and shouldn't be on top of your desk is to ask yourself the following questions:

- Which items do you use every day?
- Which items do you use at least once a week?
- Which items do you use no more than once a month?
- Are there any items—probably decorative—that you never use?

Anything you use daily stays on your desk. Items you use only once a week belong on a secondary surface. Anything you use only once a month should be placed nearby in drawers or on shelves near your desk. Items you seldom use should be stored, and items you never use should be given away or thrown out.

Many people like to personalize their offices with paperweights, photographs, awards, crafts made by their children, and other objects they enjoy. One of the nice things about a home office is that you have the freedom to include in it whatever you like. However, you need to strike a balance between a stark office with nothing but the bare necessities and one so filled with personal items there is no room in which to work. Rather than placing knickknacks on top of your desk—your prime work area—move them to another surface. By limiting the items on your desk to those that are work-related and by keeping personal items near, instead of on, your desk, you create a more functional work area. The following are the items you should keep on your desktop or primary work surface:

- Your Rolodex or other card file
- A lamp
- Your daily planner (see pages 69–70)
- A pen/pencil holder, but only if your desk has no drawers
- Your telephone, but only if your desktop is big enough

Don't automatically put your telephone on your desk. If your desk is small, you're better off putting your phone and answering machine on a surface next to your desk. If you're right-handed, put the phone to your left, and vice versa. That way you can talk on the phone and take notes without getting tangled in the cord. Avoid putting the phone behind you. Constantly swiveling around to answer it will only annoy you.

If you can, avoid using a desk blotter. A blotter is useful if you need a smooth area to write on, if your desk has a glare, or if you want to protect the wood on your desk, but it also gives you another place to stash little pieces of paper that will clutter up your work area. If you do need a desk blotter, choose one that does *not* have a calendar (most do). It's important to use only one calendar, and your blotter isn't it. If you have room in your office, use an additional work surface—either extending your desk or perpendicular to it—to hold the following items:

- Phone/answering machine, if your desk is small
- Vertical file holder, if you have no desk file drawer or if you don't want to use your desk file drawer for files
- Computer
- Printer
- Stapler and tape dispenser

If you don't have room for a secondary work surface, start thinking about shelves (see page 64) to hold the items that would otherwise be on your desk. If you keep too many items on your primary work surface, you not only make it more difficult to get down to work, but leave yourself open to accidents, such as knocking a soft drink into your computer keyboard. Get in the habit of maintaining a clear desk. If you generate a lot of mess during the day and it doesn't interfere with your productivity, that's fine, but take a few minutes before closing up shop to clear off your desktop again so that the clutter doesn't build up.

QUICK TIP FOR HOME OFFICE PROFESSIONALS

Don't blame yourself for being disorganized. Some of my clients are so ashamed of themselves they ask me to come to their offices secretly so that no one will know they needed help getting things under control. If you're disorganized, don't feel guilty. I know of no formal course in school that teaches organizing skills. How can you know something you've never been taught? Now that you have this book, I hope you'll use it to get organized to a level that suits you. You don't have to be organized to the same degree as someone else; you only have to be organized to a degree that helps you work efficiently and productively.

ORGANIZING YOUR DESK DRAWERS

In the next chapter, we'll deal with the stacks of paper that are still on your desk. Before attacking them, however, you'll need to prepare yourself for some filing. This means you need to organize your desk drawers, set up some vertical files, and buy some stacking bins.

If you look through the drawers in your desk, you may find a junk drawer or two. These are probably filled with things you didn't know where to store, so you threw them into a drawer to deal with them later. Now is the time to sort through these items and separate the useful from the useless. The following steps will take you through this process quickly:

1. Go through one drawer at a time and take out any items you haven't used in the last year. These don't belong in your immediate work area. Try to make the decision right away either to throw an item out, give it away, or store it where you can find it when you need it. Because space is probably limited, you may have to be ruthless.

2. Get rid of anything that doesn't work, including dead pens or battery-operated items that have no batteries.

3. Get a box for items you can't bear to part with. Label this box Hold. If you still haven't used the things in this box after six months, get rid of them.

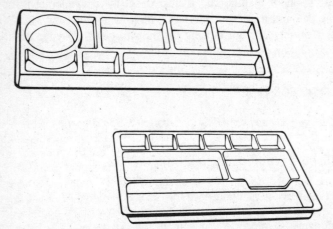

Use trays to organize small office items and keep them from tumbling together in your drawers. (Courtesy of W.T. Rogers)

4. Place all of the remaining items that you use often in a pile.

5. Measure a desk drawer to use as a place to put small things you use every day, such as pens, pencils, correction fluid, tape, scissors, and so on. (A lap drawer is best for this.) Then get dividers to fit this drawer. They will keep your supplies from rolling around every time the drawer is opened. You could also use a silverware tray or an office product designed specifically for this purpose.

6. Consider getting a drawer organizer for your stationery. These store letterhead, second sheets, and envelopes neatly in a drawer without stacking them.

7. If you have a desk file drawer, use it to hold the papers you use often. Keep the papers you are currently working on in files instead of in piles. You'll need this space for files when you start to sort through your papers (see Chapter 8).

Most desk drawers come with hanging file rods already in them. If your drawer doesn't have a frame in it, you can buy a hanging frame that is easy to assemble, or a freestanding vertical file that fits inside the drawer (see page 58). You can use either letter- or legal-size hanging folders in your drawer, but I recommend letter-size because they take up less room.

8. Now put the useful items back in your drawers, but this time organized logically. Group like items together, and store the things you use most often in closest reach. Items you use less often can be less accessible—for example, in the back of a drawer or in a bottom drawer. Items you seldom use shouldn't be in your desk, but on shelves elsewhere.

Now that you've organized everything in your desk drawers, you'll never have to waste time searching for lost items. You'll have only one place to look for each item, and you'll be able to see at a glance what you have.

WHAT TO DO IF YOUR DESK HAS NO DRAWERS

If you work at a table that has no drawers, you'll need to set up separate holders nearby for the items you use often. If possible, keep these organizers on a secondary surface, not on your desk.

Use any office organizer or divided tray to hold your pens, pencils, paper clips, and other small items. Larger organizers have room for computer

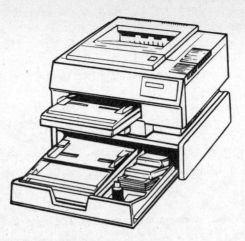

Organizers that go under your printer or fax machine make efficient use of vertical space. (Courtesy of Ring King Visibles, Inc.)

disks and other necessities. Office organizers that fit underneath your fax machine or laser printer make an efficient use of surface space.

You'll need a vertical file holder or rolling file cart in which to place paperwork you are currently working on or files you refer to often. (Current files are discussed in more detail in Chapter 8.)

There are various styles, types, and sizes of freestanding vertical file holders. One type can be used for hanging folders. Made of plastic or wire, it can be placed on your desk or on a secondary work surface. The benefits of using this type of vertical file holder is that you can use hanging folders for main filing categories and place interior folders (also called manila folders) inside for subcategories.

Another type of vertical file holder holds only interior (manila) folders. This type has a flat base with equally spaced dividers that stand vertically. Available in metal or plastic, these file holders have a couple of disadvantages: they don't give you the option of using main categories and subcategories when filing your paperwork, and when they get full it's difficult to see the labels on the folders clearly.

If you prefer using only interior (manila) file folders, I recommend that you use a tiered vertical file holder. These make it easier to see what is being filed where.

This type of freestanding vertical file holder holds hanging folders and interior folders. (Courtesy of Esselte Pendaflex Corporation)

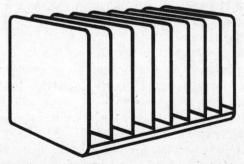

This type of freestanding vertical file holder can be used only with interior (manila) folders. (Courtesy of Globe-Weis)

Another option for freestanding vertical files is a rolling file cart. A cart lets you keep files next to your desk when you're working and away in a closet or corner when you're finished for the day or when you have to clean up your office for visitors. Rolling file carts are available in sizes small enough to fit any home office.

QUICK TIP FOR HOME OFFICE PROFESSIONALS

Avoid piles of paper at all costs! Horizontal piles of paper take up valuable surface space, distract you while you're working, and tend to grow higher and higher as you pile unrelated papers on top of one another. It's easier to find a piece of paper if it is standing vertically in a file with related papers than lying horizontally in a pile with unrelated papers. The time it takes to put papers in file folders is minimal compared to the time it takes to sort through stacks of papers—over and over—to find the ones you need.

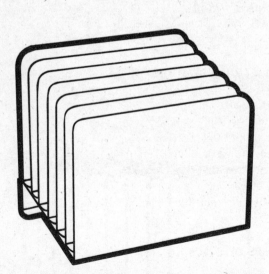

With a tiered vertical file holder, it's easier to see what is filed where. (Courtesy of Globe-Weis)

A rolling file cart provides space for hanging files without taking up desk space. (Courtesy of trav-L-file)

THE RIGHT WAY TO USE STACKING TRAYS

Traditionally people have kept stacking trays on their desks for "in" and "out" paperwork. As a home office professional, you probably don't really need "in" and "out" trays because a secretary isn't going to be processing your papers for you. In fact, it's likely that any "in" and "out" trays on your desk will turn into paperwork graveyards. There is a place in your office for stacking trays, but it isn't on your desk. Instead, use stacking trays in your supply closet to store your letterhead, stationery, envelopes, and legal pads.

THE IMPORTANCE OF STACKING BINS

There are many types of materials you may want to keep close at hand, but not on top of your desk. This material can range from articles to read, to papers that need to be filed, or even packages to mail. Instead of keeping all of this on your desk, use plastic or wire stacking bins. They are larger than

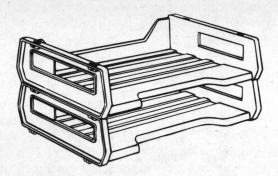

Stacking trays, useful for storing stationery or forms, don't belong on your desk. (Courtesy of W.T. Rogers)

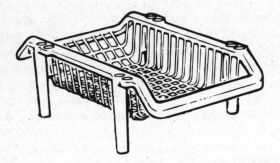

Stacking bins are essential in organizing a home office. (Courtesy of Tucker Housewares)

stacking trays and can sit on the floor, either under or next to your desk. Stacking bins are inexpensive, easy to use, and small enough to fit any office. They were originally designed to hold vegetables or toys, but they are ideal for organizing papers.

Label each stacking bin. The following are suggested categories for your stacking bins:

- *To sort.* This bin replaces your "in" box. When you bring papers into your office (for example, the mail), put them in the "to sort" bin until you're ready to process them. You should clear out your "to sort" bin by the end of each day.
- *To read.* This bin is for magazines and newspapers you don't have time to read at the moment but will read later.
- *To do.* This bin is for papers that need action. Before you put any papers in this bin, you should record any action that needs to be taken on your "to do" list (see Chapter 6).
- *To file.* Papers that need to be filed in your filing cabinet go here. Papers that should eventually be filed should not be placed on your desk or in your vertical file with papers that need immediate attention.
- *Errands.* This bin is for items you'll need to take with you when you leave the office. These could be sales information, letters to mail, papers to copy, or typing you're having done for you. Using this bin will help you avoid running out to do errands more often than necessary.

Stacking bins are also useful for large projects—for example, a photographer's stack of photographs, a salesperson's new sales materials, or an editor's book manuscripts. When used in this way, they keep large projects intact and can free up shelf space elsewhere.

Stacking bins provide a *temporary* place to store papers until you can process them. Even if you don't have time to go through them all every day, by using bins you'll know where everything is. After you've read the rest of this book and you have your paperwork and your time organized, you'll get in the habit of going through your stacking bins at least once a week.

QUICK TIP FOR HOME OFFICE PROFESSIONALS

Always try to move things ahead. It isn't realistic to think you can fully resolve within minutes every piece of paper that comes across your desk. However, you can usually find a way to move things forward if you make an immediate decision and act on it. Even if your decision is to stall, you can file a paper in your vertical files and make a note on your "to do" list to think about it later.

PUTTING YOUR WALLS TO WORK

Another way to take some of the pressure off your desk is to think vertically. Shelves, bulletin boards, and wall pockets all keep work-related materials and information nearby without taking up floor or desk space.

■ Shelves

Adding shelves above or next to your desk is an inexpensive way to gain more storage space. Prefabricated products are available that attach to the wall. Originally they were designed for corporate cubicles, but they will attach to your home office walls.

Another option is to install wall units that are long strips of sturdy plastic with shelves that hold trays for your supplies, computer disks, and anything else that would otherwise be on your desk.

■ Bulletin Boards

Bulletin boards are excellent for holding memorabilia—for example, a comic strip or a postcard from a friend. Everybody has items like this that strictly speaking don't belong in an office but are too enjoyable to throw away. A client of mine keeps "feel good" letters from satisfied clients on her bulletin board in front of her as inspiration.

People who are strongly visually oriented can use a bulletin board to keep track of long-term projects at a glance. For example, Carl, a district sales manager, didn't feel comfortable listing all of his projects on sheets of paper. He was afraid that when he filed his papers, he would forget about his projects. We solved that problem by writing on index cards all of the projects he was working on, then posting the cards on a large bulletin board. Each time Carl looked up, he could see the status of his projects. This system worked so well for him that he ended up adding his sales representatives' projects as well.

Some people would find this approach too stress-inducing. Every time you look up at the board, you realize how much there remains to be done. If this is overwhelming, you may stop looking at the board altogether. If a bulletin board would only add to your stress level, don't use it.

If you do use a bulletin board for work-related information, make sure you don't use it for "to do" reminders or important papers that need action. If you use your bulletin board to supplement your "to do" list (see Chapter 6), these tasks will start to fall through the cracks. The longer notes to yourself stay posted on your bulletin board, the more likely it is that you'll just stop seeing them. Your brain will tune them out because they have been there so long they become meaningless. To use a bulletin board effectively, I recommend the following:

- Hang the board on the wall, rather than keeping it propped up against the wall.
- If you use a bulletin board to track projects, divide it vertically into columns and label each column.
- At the end of each month, review the entire board and remove information that is no longer valid.
- When you no longer refer to anything on the board, take it down and throw or file it away.

An alternative to a bulletin board is a white board. These boards come in a wide range of sizes, with a special marker that easily wipes off with a cloth. Some come with a preprinted, permanent monthly calendar, a weekly calendar, or blanks in which to fill in tasks to do. These work well for people who plan multiple events or who need to track several projects at the same time.

Another alternative is a magnetic board. You type or write the tasks or projects you want to track on cards (the cards are available in various sizes), then insert the cards into magnetic holders that stick to the board. This option gives you the flexibility of moving tasks forward as you work on a project. Other boards have pockets that hold index cards; all you have to do is move cards from pocket to pocket. Whatever type of board you choose, make sure it is helping you be more productive instead of distracting you or providing a dumping ground for miscellaneous papers.

■ Wall Pockets

Wall pockets, or "hot files," are plastic holders that hang on the wall to hold papers, supplies, or anything else you need to have within reach. Wall pockets can hold about 100 sheets of paper, or four to five interior folders. Many people aren't aware that they can use this office organizing trick to sort and store paperwork they refer to often.

Sally, a representative for a line of clothing, told me during one of my seminars that she had trouble keeping track of her price sheets. She constantly received calls from clients asking her what the latest prices were, and she had to call them back after she'd found her pricing sheets. First I suggested that she use a notebook, but she already had several notebooks for other purposes and didn't have room to store another. That's when I suggested that she use a wall pocket to hold the price sheets. She agreed that this would give her quick access to her papers near the phone without taking up extra space in her home office.

MORE CHEAP TRICKS

Look everywhere for products that might suit your needs. Many items can be used for purposes other than those for which they were intended.

- A horizontal shoe sorter with spaces for nine pairs of shoes ($8\frac{1}{2}'' \times 11''$) makes a perfectly adequate place in which to store forms or sales sheets.
- A large kitchen trash can makes the best office wastebasket because a small one increases the amount of time you spend emptying the trash. Hint: trash can liners make it easier to empty your office trash quickly.
- A silverware tray makes a perfect drawer divider.
- Use a magazine holder, laid on its side, to store envelopes and letterhead vertically.

QUICK TIP FOR HOME OFFICE PROFESSIONALS

Keep the items you use often within reach. Constantly retrieving items you use a lot is as big a time waster as searching for lost items. Every time you leave your desk, you waste time and become distracted. It's important to keep in mind that wasted minutes each day turn into wasted hours each week. Those wasted hours will cost money.

USE A WORK CIRCLE

Before deciding where to put all of your office items, sit at your desk and imagine a circle around yourself. To make the most productive use of both your office equipment and your time, the items you will need on a regular basis should be stored in easy reach within that circle.

Are you always reaching into a cabinet or closet to get your adding machine? Make it more accessible. Are there books or papers you refer to often? Keep them within arm's reach of your desk. Anticipate the reasons you leave your desk, then try to find a way to eliminate the problem.

Most people are astonished to find out how much time they waste retrieving items that are lost or inconveniently placed. The following chart will help you gauge how effectively your office is meeting your needs. For one week, keep track of the number of times you leave your desk to search for something you've misplaced or to get something you need. After you've filled in this chart, you'll see not only how often you're interrupted, but what needs to be corrected within your office.

Wasted Time Chart

Week of_____

Troublesome Item	Item Lost	Item Out of Reach
_____	☐	☐
_____	☐	☐
_____	☐	☐
_____	☐	☐
_____	☐	☐
_____	☐	☐
	☐	☐

6

CREATING YOUR OWN PLANNING NOTEBOOK

A problem I often see in home offices is lists and little scraps of paper everywhere—taped to the walls, stuck to the phone, pinned to the bulletin board, buried under paperwork. These little pieces of paper are sometimes all over the home—in the kitchen, by an upstairs phone, stuck to the refrigerator. I've seen "to do" lists taped to front doors, phone numbers stuck to mirrors, and reminders fluttering from computer terminals.

Ours is an information society. We're bombarded constantly with facts, figures, and ideas. We're also an achievement-oriented society, heavily burdened with obligations, tasks, and deadlines. We have a lot on our minds, and it can be difficult to keep everything straight.

When an important piece of information comes to your attention, your instinct is to grab the first piece of paper available and write down what needs to be done or remembered. The husband of a friend of mine, a cabinet-maker, told me that he writes notes to himself on blocks of wood, in that he has more wood in his work area than paper. They do the trick, all right, but they're difficult to file!

What's the solution? Keep a planning notebook in which you record and organize all of this information. A planning notebook allows you to do all of your planning in one place. It is your planning control center: it tells you what you need to do and how to find the information you need to do what needs to be done.

If you custom-design your own planner, it will meet your needs exactly. In the next chapter, we'll look at some alternatives, but please read this chapter first so that you understand the full importance of using some sort of personal planning system.

HOW TO DESIGN A CUSTOMIZED PLANNING NOTEBOOK

You can easily and inexpensively customize a notebook to fit your needs. To create your own planning notebook, follow these guidelines.

1. *Select a three-ring binder in a size you like.* Your planner can be an inexpensive vinyl binder or an expensive, zippered leather case. Decide if you want a binder that holds 8½″ × 11″ pages or a smaller size. The size you choose depends in part on how you are going to carry your planner. If you are going to take it with you in a briefcase, you may want the larger size. If you want to keep your planner in your purse or jacket, choose a smaller size.

2. *Add as many subject dividers as you need.* Label the tabs with the headings that follow that are appropriate for you. I recommend that you start with at least the following:

- Current projects
- Monthly calendar
- To do

Then add whatever categories from the following list that you would find useful:

- Addresses/phone numbers
- Books
- Client status
- Communication
- Expenses
- Future tasks
- Goals

- Ideas
- Notes
- Personal
- Phone calls
- Reference
- Travel

3. *Add sheets for each section.* Some sections—for example, your "to do" sheets—will require a certain format. You can easily draw up original forms and run off copies for your planner. (Remember to allow space in the margin for the binder ring holes.)

THE "TO DO" SECTION

"To do" sheets are a critical part of any planning notebook, whether you choose a commercially available planner or custom design your own.

QUICK TIP FOR HOME OFFICE PROFESSIONALS

Maintaining a daily or weekly "to do" list is absolutely essential. Studies show that the day you start using a "to do" list you become 25 percent more effective. A "to do" list not only shows what you need to do, but shows what you are and are not accomplishing each day. More than a random list of things to remember, your "to do" list helps you organize your time and work more efficiently. If you positively can't stand "to do" lists, use another personal organizing system that will help you keep track of your obligations and accomplishments.

■ The Importance of a "To Do" List

When you work at home, it's easy to write a note at one phone, jot down a reminder in your family room, and make another note to yourself in the kitchen—and not bring any of these scraps of paper into your office. Even within your office, you may stick one reminder to your answering machine, another to a file folder, and a third to your desk lamp. You end up both losing those pieces of paper and losing track of the big picture: all of the things you need to do.

A "to do" list is the key to getting and staying organized, which is in turn the key to being maximally effective every day. With a "to do" list, you keep your goals in sight hour by hour; you know not only what you need to do, but when you need to do it.

Not using a "to do" list creates a Catch-22 situation: you're too busy to create a list, but you know that using the list would keep you from being so busy. Some people who are strongly task-oriented feel it takes less time to perform a task than to write it down. Whatever your rationale, if you don't use a "to do" list, you are failing to take advantage of an essential organizing tool. When you eventually start using a "to do" list, you'll realize why it enables you to work so much more effectively.

A "to do" list helps you set priorities and focus on important tasks. Part of creating an effective "to do" list is organizing your tasks in order of importance. By writing down all of the jobs that need to be done and then tackling the most important ones first, you guarantee that you will actually make progress every day.

It helps you control your day, instead of letting your day control you. A big time waster is being in the position of always reacting to situations as they occur instead of creating opportunities to get things done. One of my clients, a retired bank president, told me that he never used to plan his day. He would react to the first crisis that hit his desk and that would set the pace for the rest of his day. When he was in a corporate office, he felt he never had time to plan ahead because he was always "putting out fires." Now that he was in a home office, he had the time to plan ahead, but he had never learned how. He started using a "to do" list and soon got in the habit of listing all of the situations that required his attention and arranging them in order of urgency. Instead of constantly being a fire fighter, he now sets his own goals and accomplishes them.

A "to do" list enables you to be flexible without losing control of your day. A sudden interruption can totally disrupt the direction of your workday. A "to do" list gets you back on track when things aren't going according to plan.

It organizes your day. With a "to do" list, you can handle tasks when you feel like handling them. Suppose a good time for you to make phone calls is late in the day. By writing down all of the calls you need to make and running them all at once, you have uninterrupted time to work in the morning.

A "to do" list takes the strain off your memory. If you're constantly trying to remember tasks to do, calls to make, and appointments to keep, you not only live an unnecessarily anxious life but have little time for creative thinking.

Tom, a sales rep, told me he was "cursed" with an excellent memory. He didn't need to write anything down because he could remember everything—his appointments, directions to appointments, calls to make, samples to replenish. I persuaded Tom to use a "to do" list anyway, and he discovered that when he wrote down all of the information he'd been juggling in his mind all day, he was able to think more creatively.

It helps you keep your desk clear. A "to do" list is an important tool for managing paper. First of all, it replaces all of those scraps of paper mentioned earlier. Second, it helps you organize your work papers. When used correctly, a "to do" list directs you to any piece of paper you need when you need it. If you use a "to do" list in conjunction with filing papers where they belong, your paperwork will be organized and your desktop will be clear, which helps you focus on one task at a time.

It helps prevent oversights. With a "to do" list, you're much less likely to let things slip through the cracks. Better still, you'll record any follow-up action that needs to be taken at a later date, which eliminates the need for all of those reminders stuck to your calendar.

Get in the habit of writing down all of the tasks you need to accomplish, both short- and long-term. You'll take a load off your memory, and you'll get more done. Using a "to do" list is a new habit that takes time to acquire. Your level of desire will determine how quickly you assume this new habit. It's definitely a habit worth acquiring.

QUICK TIP FOR HOME OFFICE PROFESSIONALS

Use adhesive-backed notes in moderation. Instead of using them for reminders, use them to write quick notes on papers you send to someone else, or to indicate on your paperwork where documents should be filed. When you need to write yourself a reminder, add it to your "to do" list. Avoid keeping any pads of paper on your desk. Use your planner instead.

■ Establishing Priorities

The most important tip to using your "to do" list effectively is to organize your tasks and calls in their order of importance. After you've written down everything you need to accomplish, use either letters or numbers to rank your tasks and calls from urgent (do today), to important (do soon), to if possible (do eventually). Doing this helps you focus on those activities you need to handle first.

If you number your list, the top-priority task is 1, the next most urgent is 2, and so on. If you letter your tasks, break them into three groups: highest priority, which you identify with the letter A; second priority, which you label B; and lowest priority, or C. You can further refine this by numbering the tasks within each group—A1, A2, A3—to indicate their relative level of importance.

Whichever method you choose, concentrate on your top priority items first until they are completed. If your priorities change, renumber (or reletter) your list. If you're having trouble determining which tasks are most important, decide which are money-making tasks that will enable you to increase your income.

If your "to do" list—tasks and phone calls—runs longer than fifteen entries, evaluate whether certain tasks could be done at a later date. If your list becomes unmanageably long, it will stop being helpful. In addition, the longer you make your list, the more likely you will be to put off working on tasks.

You will have tasks on your list that are not a high priority, yet may take you only a few minutes to do. It's tempting to do these tasks first. If you know that a certain item will only take a few minutes to do and it's weighing heavily on your mind, do it. For example, if there's an article on your desk that you want to send someone, take a minute to address the envelope and put it with your other letters to mail. The key words are "a few minutes." Avoid small tasks that will eventually take more than half an hour and that were never a high priority.

QUICK TIP FOR HOME OFFICE PROFESSIONALS

Focus on your top-priority tasks every day before working on less urgent tasks. If you are able to accomplish your number one tasks, then you've had a productive day. Strive for a balance between quality and quantity.

■ Updating Your "To Do" List

As you complete a task, cross it off your list for that day. One woman I know even went so far as to use a stamp that read "completed" to indicate the tasks she had accomplished. She needed that extra sense of accomplishment to get her through her daily list. Some people get such satisfaction from crossing things off their list that they will do tasks that weren't listed, then write them down so that they can cross them off.

At the end of each day, transfer any item you didn't complete to the next day's list or to a "to do" list for a later date. Then cross these items off your list for that day. It's important to move these tasks forward so that you don't have to flip back to previous lists.

If you find yourself constantly transferring the same "to do's," use a master project list. Look at it at the beginning of each week, pull tasks from it, and enter these tasks on days when you will be able to do them.

■ Finding a Format That Works for You

There are many ways to design a daily "to do" sheet, but all have the day's date, or a place to put the date, at the top. Most have blank lines to the left, in which to record your tasks to do and calls to make, and an hour-by-hour breakdown of the day on the right. Even if you don't have many appointments, the hourly chart can help you block out times to work on certain tasks.

There's nothing wrong with putting your personal tasks on your "to do" list. However, list them under separate headings, such as "personal," "personal tasks to do," and "personal calls."

TO DO

_____
_____
_____
_____
_____
_____
_____
_____
_____
_____
_____

TO CALL

_____
_____
_____
_____
_____
_____
_____
_____
_____
_____
_____

PERSONAL

_____
_____
_____
_____
_____
_____
_____

	APPOINTMENTS FOR _____
6:00	
6:30	
7:00	
7:30	
8:00	
8:30	
9:00	
9:30	
10:00	
10:30	
11:00	
11:30	
12:00	
12:30	
1:00	
1:30	
2:00	
2:30	
3:00	
3:30	
4:00	
4:30	
5:00	
5:30	
6:00	
6:30	
7:00	
7:30	
8:00	
8:30	
9:00	
9:30	
10:00	

Try this format for your daily "to do" sheets in your personal planner.

■ Using a Weekly "To Do" List

Some people don't need a daily "to do" list, but are sufficiently organized with a weekly "to do" list. A weekly "to do" list provides spaces for you to write down what you need to do and the day of the week on which you should do it.

If you use a weekly "to do" list, treat it the same way you would a daily list. Cross off the tasks you accomplish, and at the end of each week transfer any remaining items to a sheet for the week when you will be able to handle them.

■ Filling in Your Planner's "To Do" Section

Once you hit on an approach that works for you, make sure you have enough daily or weekly "to do" lists for three months. This way you can note on the appropriate sheets any tasks to be performed in the days or weeks ahead. Don't keep more than three months' worth of sheets or your planner will get too full. (Tasks to be accomplished more than three months in the future will go in your planner's monthly calendar section.)

When you open your planner, your "to do" sheet should be on the left, and a blank sheet of paper should be on the right, facing your "to do" sheet. (You can reverse these if you wish; the important thing is to have these two sheets facing each other.) Use the "to do" sheet to itemize your tasks, and use the other sheet to record miscellaneous information for that day (for example, a phone number, directions to an appointment, or your business mileage). At the end of the day, make sure you transfer any useful information from your "miscellaneous" sheet to the correct files in your office.

It's also a good idea to record on the "miscellaneous" sheets any actions you take during the day. One client of mine recently saved himself from having to take a client of his to court by having recorded in his planner all of the activities he performed for his clients. When one of his clients threatened not to pay him, he showed the client that he had maintained written records of everything he had done, and he indicated that he would be ready, if necessary, to produce these records in court. The client paid.

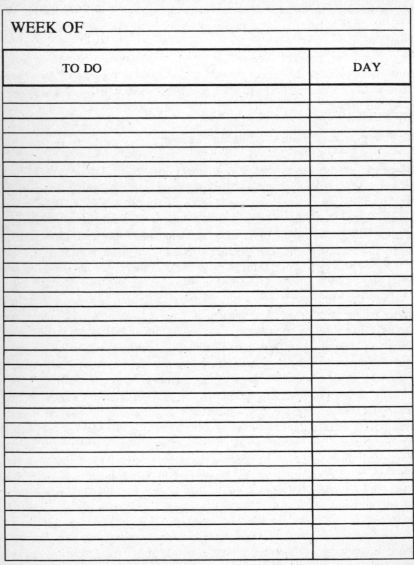

An alternative to a daily "to do" sheet is a weekly "to do" sheet like this one.

■ Storing Old "To Do" Lists

When you are finished with a month's worth of "to do" lists, if they're still legible, store them in a binder in case you need to refer to them again. You may find yourself going back to them to track down a mileage figure or a phone number. Throw them away if you know you'll never refer to them again. Keep in mind, however, my client who avoided going to court!

THE MONTHLY CALENDAR SECTION

In this section of your planner, put an entire year's worth of monthly calendars. Make sure the squares on your calendars are big enough to actually write in. Some are so small that only one appointment will fit in each square.

Your "to do" list is for recording tasks to do, while your monthly calendar is for recording appointments. Whenever you schedule an appointment, write it down on the correct monthly calendar. You may also want to record the appointment on the hourly section of your "to do" list, if you don't always refer to your monthly calendar. Your monthly calendar will give you an overview of each month, while your daily sheet (if it has a place for appointments) will give you an overview of each day. If you're scheduling an appointment that will take place some time during the next three months—remember, you have three months' worth of "to do" sheets—record the appointment on your monthly calendar. If you're scheduling an appointment further ahead than that, write it on the correct monthly calendar. You want to avoid the possibility of forgetting an appointment because you didn't refer to your monthly calendar.

The only time you should use a calendar to record tasks is when you don't have "to do" sheets in your daily planner for a future month. For example, if it is May, and someone wants you to call him in September, you would write that on your September calendar, in pencil. When you add the September "to do" sheets to your planner, you would transfer this note to the appropriate day's "to do" sheet, then erase it from the calendar and use the September calendar for appointments only.

Use only one calendar to record appointments. You'll reduce the likelihood of missing or double-booking appointments. You could use a wall calendar for reference only—not to record appointments.

THE CURRENT PROJECTS SECTION

This is a master list of all projects you currently have in progress. List the project, a brief description, and a deadline date. When you complete a project, cross it off your list.

This master list will serve as an overview of everything you need to accomplish. When you take the time to write down all of the projects you're currently working on, they will seem less overwhelming. Each week, look at this list and transfer items that need to be accomplished to the appropriate "to do" lists for the week.

THE FUTURE TASKS SECTION

Use this section to list all of the tasks you would like to accomplish in the future but not on any particular day. Writing them down will take them out of your mind and leave you free to think about the tasks at hand. Look at this list periodically, and when you're ready to work on something, take it off the list and put it on a "to do" sheet.

A future tasks list is helpful in taking some of the pressure off your immediate "to do" lists. An attendee of one of my seminars showed me a computer printout of his "to do" list, and he had seventy-six tasks on the list! When he didn't get to all of them each day (which obviously would be impossible), the tasks would automatically transfer to the next day's list. This was all very organized, but not very helpful. I suggested that he create a future task list for his long-term tasks, and that he put on his daily list only the tasks he needed to do immediately. He could then refer to his future task list each week and transfer selected items to his daily "to do" lists. This made his daily lists much more manageable and enabled him to track his top-priority tasks more effectively.

THE CLIENT STATUS SECTION

Use this section to make notes about conversations you have with various clients. You could use the page facing your daily "to do" list for this purpose, but a separate client status section in your planner enables you to keep a client status sheet for each client.

Some people like to keep client status sheets in their planner, rather than filing them in their client files after every talk. This way they can maintain a running account of their conversations that they can carry with them. Then, when they are waiting for a client in his or her office or in a restaurant, they can prepare themselves by reviewing their discussions.

When you're in your office and speaking with a client, reach for your planner and record the date, time, and the highlights of your conversation on the appropriate client status sheet. By using a client status sheet, you'll eliminate the need for scraps of paper to record notes from a conversation.

When you're out of your office and speaking to a client, either in person or over the phone, the same rule applies. Jot down the important points of your conversation on the appropriate sheet.

THE IDEAS SECTION

Sometimes when you least expect it you get a great idea or a solution to a problem that has been bothering you for weeks. Usually that idea will come to you at an awkward time—at a restaurant, in a meeting, or while driving your car. Wherever you are, you need to have one place to put those ideas. You may not be able to act on these ideas right away, but at least you'll know where to find them when you need them: in the ideas section of your planner.

THE GOALS SECTION

Some people lack a sense of direction because they don't have well-defined goals. Others are afraid to write down their goals for fear they may actually achieve them. Still others are so busy with day-to-day concerns that they stop even trying to think about where they are headed.

QUICK TIP FOR HOME OFFICE PROFESSIONALS

Take the time to write down your goals, both long- and short-term. For a home office professional, clearly defined goals are essential. No one else is tracking your progress. If you don't know where you're going, how will you know you're on the right track? If you don't pay attention to how much you are doing, how can you be sure you're accomplishing anything?

CLIENT STATUS

COMPANY:			
CONTACT:			TITLE:
ADDRESS:			
PHONE NUMBER:			

DATE	TYPE OF CONTACT (Phone/Letter)	ACTIVITY LOG	ACTION TO BE TAKEN

Using a client status sheet like this one helps you keep track of your conversations with clients.

It's important to write down specific goals you want to accomplish. Follow these guidelines when setting your goals.

1. *Make your goals realistic.* If you are currently earning $25,000 per year, it may not be reasonable to make $100,000 your goal for next year. Instead, you could set a goal of increasing your income by 25 or 50 percent.

2. *Make your goals specific.* For example, rather than writing down, "Make more money next year," give a specific percentage or dollar amount. This automatically gives you a better way of measuring your performance.

3. *Be flexible about your goals.* Situations change, and a goal that might have seemed appropriate at one time may become less important or less feasible with time. Be willing to change your goals, if necessary, in that clinging to an outmoded goal is counterproductive.

I have developed a simple goal planner that will help you map out your goals. Take out a blank sheet of paper that will fit into your planner and copy the format of the goal planner on pages 83–84. Then fill in your personal ambitions.

If you realize that a particular goal is going to take longer than you thought, don't drop it from your goal planner altogether. Instead, just move it up a notch so that it's in a more distant category.

Goals are powerful tools that will help you build a successful business. Take the time to commit your goals to paper. Look at your goals at least once a week. At the three-month, six-month, and one-year points, see how close you have come to achieving them. You will be surprised at how much you are able to accomplish in a short amount of time.

The tasks you put on your "to do" list each day or each week should be directly related to your goals. If what you do each day doesn't relate to your lifetime goals, then either change your tasks or change your goals.

GOAL PLANNER

Lifetime Goals   (Add today's date)

In this section, write down everything you would like to accomplish over your entire career. Don't censor yourself; write down anything that comes to mind.

One-Year Goals   (Add the date in one year)

List here the steps you will need to take to achieve your lifetime goals. For example, if your lifetime goal is to become an expert in your field, your one-year goal may be to read one book a week in that field.

Six-Month Goals   (Add the date in six months)

In this section, list goals you could accomplish in six months to help you achieve your lifetime goals.

Three-Month Goals   (Add the date in three months)

List here the short-term goals that could help you achieve your lifetime goals.

THE ADDRESSES/PHONE NUMBERS SECTION

If you have ever been away from your office and needed a particular phone number but didn't have it and couldn't get it, you'll know how helpful this section can be. Design your own address/phone number sheets, copy as many as you need, and organize them in your planner either alphabetically or by category.

This section works in conjunction with the phone card file that sits on your desk. If you pick up an address or phone number during the day, remember to add it to your desk file.

Some people use only their planner for addresses and phone numbers. This works well until you have too many addresses and phone numbers to fit into this section. When that happens, limit the listings in your planner to the numbers you use most often, and use a card file in your office for your entire listing. If others need access to your phone numbers, you'll definitely have to keep a complete listing in your office.

Another option is to computerize your list by using a client-based software program such as Telemagic or ACT! (see page 195). With a client tracking program you can print out the names and phone numbers of your clients to take with you while you are out of the office. You have the capability of printing out the names of your clients by zip code, city, state, name, and so on.

THE BOOKS SECTION

It seems that wherever I go or whatever I read, someone recommends a book. Whenever anyone gives me the title of a book, I turn to the books section of my planner and write it down. Then I take my planner with me when I go to the bookstore. A book list works the same way as an office supplies list: it helps you focus on the books you want to buy and keeps you from buying books on impulse.

A woman in one of my seminars told me that she used to go to the bookstore every week just to browse, but that she always managed to leave with a new book. When her bookcase started overflowing, she sorted through her books, took out the ones she had never read and knew she wouldn't read, and sold them to a used-book bookstore. Now she keeps a list of books to read and goes into a bookstore with a purpose. She is saving money by not buying books she will never read.

It doesn't really matter how you decide to list your books, so choose a format that works for you. You can list the books you want to read by category (for example, sales, marketing, public relations, or motivation), or you can list them in alphabetical order by title. Listing them alphabetically by author is another possibility, but this can get frustrating because people sometimes remember the title of a book but not the author's name. Whichever approach you decide on, use it consistently.

After you buy a book on your list, put a checkmark next to it. After you've read it, highlight its listing.

THE PHONE CALLS SECTION

Depending on the company you work for or clients you work with, you may need to keep track of long distance phone calls in order to get reimbursed. You may even get paid for the time you spend on certain calls. Either way, you need a place to record these calls.

A phone sheet makes it easier for you to sort out your phone bill when it arrives. All you need to do is compare your bill with your list and you can quickly tell which calls are personal and which are business-related.

Make up some phone sheets in a format that suits your needs. Include a column for the date, name of the person called, his or her company, and the phone number.

Whenever you make a long distance call or a call to an important client, reach for your planner. Your list will serve as an accurate record of when you called someone, so that when you speak again, you can refer with precision to the previous phone call you made on a certain date.

THE TRAVEL SECTION

If you do a lot of driving around, you need to keep records of your business mileage for tax purposes. You can scribble this information opposite your "to do" list, or you can make up travel pages for your planner. Include columns for the date, point of departure, destination, and the number of miles traveled. Again, the idea is to avoid using miscellaneous scraps of paper to record this information.

THE EXPENSES SECTION

The requirements for verifying expenses with the IRS leave little room for error. Keep accurate track of your expenses by using an expense sheet. Expense sheets are easy to draw up; follow these steps.

1. Take a blank sheet of paper that fits into your planner and divide it into four vertical columns that start two inches from the top of the page and run down to the bottom.
2. At the top of the first column, write Date.
3. At the top of the second column, write Type of Expense.
4. At the top of the third column, write Amount Spent.
5. The last heading should read, Reimbursable. Under this heading, you'll write either "yes" or "no."

In addition to expense sheets, you will need to put in this section of your planner a small manila envelope or a plastic zippered pocket with three holes in it to hold receipts during the day. Whenever you incur a business-related expense, enter it on your expense sheet, and then file the receipt in the envelope or pocket. Transfer your receipts to your office files at the end of each day so that they don't build up inside your planning notebook.

Recording your expenses takes a little extra time, but it will save time when you start preparing your tax returns because you'll have a running list of expenses to refer to. Also, in the unfortunate event of an audit, you'll be glad you did it.

THE COMMUNICATION SECTION

Throughout the day, you may think of things you want to mention to your clients, spouse, or staff. Instead of calling them every time you have something to say, keep a running list of items to discuss.

This section of your planner works best if you keep a separate sheet for each person with whom you are in touch. At the top of each page, write the name of the individual with whom you want to discuss certain points. As you think of other ideas, add them to your list. When you're ready to make the call, refer to your planner.

Using a communication sheet leaves your mind free to concentrate on other tasks. It also guarantees that you won't find yourself saying, "There's something else I want to tell you, but I can't think of it."

THE NOTES SECTION

As a home office professional, you probably attend fewer meetings than your corporate counterparts. Probably the only meetings you attend are with clients. Still, these meetings may generate pages and pages of notes. The next time you're in a meeting, instead of taking notes on legal pads, turn to this section and take notes.

There is an art to taking notes. Your planner can help you make the most of your meeting and can help you make sure you follow up on everything discussed.

1. At the top of a blank piece of paper, write the date and the type of meeting (i.e., staff meeting or client meeting).
2. Draw an "action box" in the righthand corner of the page. As you take notes during the meeting, record any action that needs to be taken in the action box. For example, if you need to send information to someone or write a follow-up letter to a client, make a note in the action box.
3. After the meeting, transfer the information from the action box to your "to do" sheets. Then file the rest of your notes in the appropriate file. (This depends on how you have organized your office files. Notes from a

client meeting may be filed under the client's name, whereas notes from a staff meeting may be kept in a staff meeting notebook.)

THE REFERENCE SECTION

Use this section as a catchall for information. The listings within your planner's reference section could include the following:

- Pricing information for your products
- Condensed dictionary (these are available in 8½″ × 11″ pages and smaller)
- Dates to remember (birthdays or special occasions for family members or clients)
- Office supply list for your next trip to the office supply store
- Directions to places you don't go to often, but need to know how to find

THE PERSONAL SECTION

Use this section to record information about personal projects, hobbies, or activities. You can also insert a sheet for each member of your family.

GETTING STARTED

Using a planning notebook and keeping all of the information you receive in one place is a new habit. For the first twenty-four hours after you design your planner, don't write a single note to yourself on a scrap of paper. Instead, record any information you get or need in your planning notebook in the appropriate section.

Use the chart that follows as a reference guide to storing information within your planning notebook.

Type of Information	Where It Goes
A client's new phone number and address.	In the addresses/phone numbers section.
Request from a client for product samples and/or literature.	On your "to do" list for a particular day.
A phone message with the number of a client who wants you to call back in three months.	In the monthly calendar section, in pencil, on the day you plan to place the call.
Receipt from lunch with a client.	Record lunch on expense sheet in expenses section; file receipt in envelope.
Directions to a new client's office.	On the sheet facing the daily "to do" sheet for that day's appointment. (Or, in reference section, if you have one.)
Note to yourself that you tried to reach someone and left a message.	Next to the entry on your "to do" list, write "mess" to show that you have left a message. On your "to do" list for the next day, write, "should hear from (whoever it is)."

If any of the previous information was given to you on a slip of paper, toss out the slip after recording the information (with the exception of the lunch receipt). No more little scraps of paper!

DO IT YOUR WAY

Some type of planning system is essential in getting and staying organized. I usually recommend that clients create their own planners if they haven't found one that fits their needs. However, there are other approaches that may work for you. We'll discuss these in the next chapter.

7

OTHER
PERSONAL PLANNING
SYSTEMS

There is no one-size-fits-all method for personal organizing. Some people can't be bothered with custom-designing a planning notebook, or need only a simple notebook. Others hate "to do" lists and prefer working with actual papers. Some people don't mind working with "to do" lists, but they become impatient with having to write them out every day. Still others prefer to get organized by writing notes to themselves on index cards.

Whatever your preferences are, there is a personal planning system that will suit your needs. In addition to designing your own planning notebook (see Chapter 6), your options include the following:

- Using a spiral notebook
- Computerized planning
- Electronic pocket organizers
- Using a commercially available planner
- Using tickler files

Any of these systems will provide you with an efficient way to keep track of tasks.

USING A SPIRAL NOTEBOOK TO PLAN

If you need only a place to record tasks to do and calls to make, a spiral notebook is a good alternative to a planning notebook. A good friend of mine used to write notes to herself on her hand. In that she is a physician and washes her hands many times a day, this method wasn't always successful. Now she uses a small spiral notebook that fits in her coat pocket. Here is a step-by-step way to set up and use a spiral notebook.

1. Decide if you want to use a spiral notebook that is bound on the side or one that is bound at the top. Spiral notebooks are available in a wide variety of sizes; pick one that works for you.
2. At the top of each page, put every day and date for the next three months. (If you are planning by the week, write "week of . . ." and fill in the dates.) Although you could save paper by entering dates on both the front and back of the pages, you probably will want to enter a date only on the front and leave the back for notes.
3. Divide each page in half, either horizontally or vertically, and label one section "to do" and the other "calls." You could also add sections labeled "personal" to record your personal tasks and calls.
4. In the "to do" section write all of the tasks you need to accomplish, and in the "calls" section write all of the calls you need to make. Organize your tasks and calls according to their level of importance, as was described earlier (see page 74).
5. At the end of each day, transfer the items that you weren't able to accomplish that day to the next day's list or to a list a few days later. Then cross the items off that day's list and move forward to the next page.

Don't use your spiral notebook to schedule appointments. Instead, use a pocket calendar or desk calendar in conjunction with your spiral notebook. This way you can see all of your obligations at a glance and you'll be less likely to make scheduling errors.

QUICK TIP FOR HOME OFFICE PROFESSIONALS

*Out of sight is **not** out of mind.* Many people keep too many papers on their desk because they are afraid of forgetting about them if they file them away. Keep your tasks in mind by writing them down on your "to do" list before you file away your documents. You'll always have a reminder at hand—without the clutter.

COMPUTERIZED PLANNING

There are many computer programs available to help you plan your days. Part of the attraction of these programs is that, depending on the program, your computer can automatically transfer items that haven't been accomplished to a new "to do" list. However, some people switch from manually planning their days to using a computer only to find that they are no more organized than before.

A computer will not automatically organize you. It's a tool, like any other tool or product. You need to have a basic understanding of how to get organized the old-fashioned way before you can completely depend upon a computer to help you plan each day.

How do you decide if it's worthwhile to purchase a planning program? Consider the following factors before investing:

1. Is your computer always on during the day? If not, you are less likely to take advantage of computerized planning, which involves printing out daily planning sheets at the beginning of each day.
2. Are you out of your office more than you are in it? If you aren't near your computer, it can't help you. A planning notebook has the advantage of being portable.
3. Would you keep your computerized "to do" lists current, taking off the items you've accomplished and adding new tasks to do and calls to make? If you find entering these adjustments a bother, computerized planning won't help you get organized.

ELECTRONIC POCKET ORGANIZERS

Small, hand-held electronic pocket organizers completely eliminate the need for paper in scheduling tasks and appointments. Some people find electronic organizers awkward to use at first because you look at a screen instead of a piece of paper, but this is actually their great advantage.

Electronic pocket organizers have a variety of functions, including the following:

- Calendar
- Schedule
- Telephone numbers and addresses
- Calculator
- Memo
- Privacy feature
- Optional computer interface to back up the information you have entered

You can also add software cards to increase the functions of an electronic organizer.

Martin, a home-based sales rep for a long-distance company, made fun of a colleague with an electronic planner who worked in the corporate office. Whenever A. J. heard a new piece of information or was reminded of something he needed to do, he would whip out his pocket organizer. Martin thought this was hilarious, until A. J. pointed out that Martin was always calling him for phone numbers and meeting dates. Martin went out and bought his own electronic organizer, and found that it worked better for him than his old planning notebook because he was more likely to take it with him wherever he went.

The following is a summary of the advantages and disadvantages of using a pocket organizer:

Advantages

Keeps all of the information you need in one very compact place.

Extremely portable; fits easily in a purse or briefcase.

Interfaces with your computer so that you can back up information.

Ideal for people with poor hand-writing.

Disadvantages

Small screen display may be hard to read.

Must be careful not to drop it.

Not easy to enter information if you have large fingers.

If you forget to change the battery, you lose everything. (However, adapters are available; also, the organizer will warn you when the battery is running low.)

QUICK TIP FOR HOME OFFICE PROFESSIONALS

Take the time to equip yourself with whatever you need to get organized. This could mean buying anything from a new planner to a new computer. If you don't have the right equipment, you are making your work life unnecessarily difficult. By equipping yourself with the right products, you'll save time and money, and you'll improve the service you give your clients.

USING A COMMERCIALLY AVAILABLE PLANNER

You may decide you want to use one of the predesigned planners available on the market. Planners range in price from $25 to over $200 and come in a wide variety of sizes and formats.

Different planners have different unique features that you might find useful. Some include plastic pockets for credit cards. Some have wrap-around "to do" lists. Some use cards that flip up for viewing instead of pages that turn. The Franklin Planner, available in various sizes and bindings, has a place for your tasks, appointments, and expenses on one page and a place for notes on the facing page.

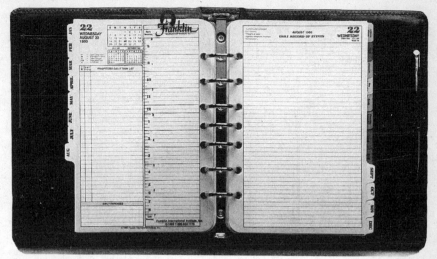

A loose-leaf Franklin Planner.

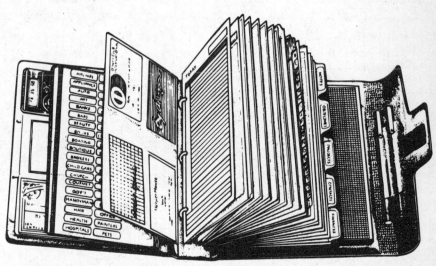

The Day Runner planner.

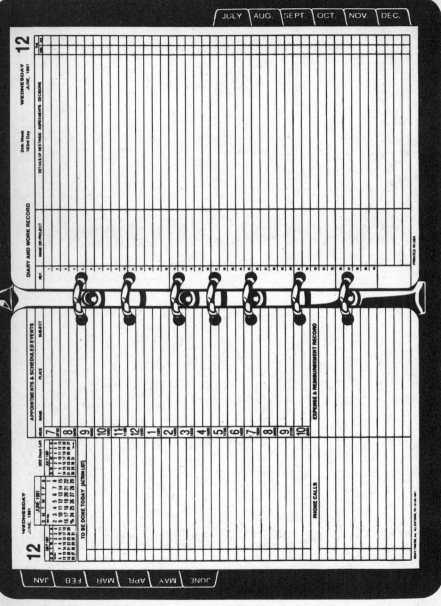

The Day-Timers planner.

The Day Runner comes with preprinted and blank labels to help you customize your planner. There are also clear pockets that hold credit cards and business cards, as well as a space for your checkbook.

With a Day-Timers planner, each planning page includes an "action list," a phone calls list, an hourly breakdown of the day, and a place to record expenses. On the facing page you have room to record notes about projects.

The Time/Design planner includes a wraparound "to do" list. Instead of rewriting your list each day, you simply turn the page and fold your list over.

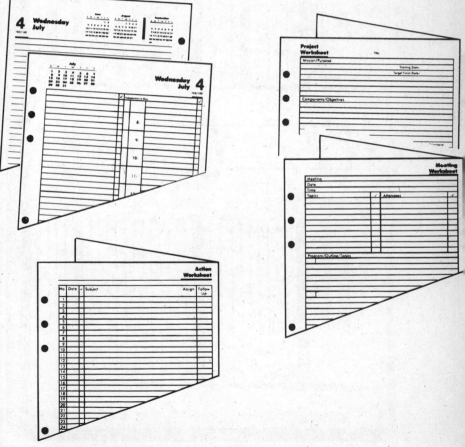

Time/Design with a wraparound "to do" list.

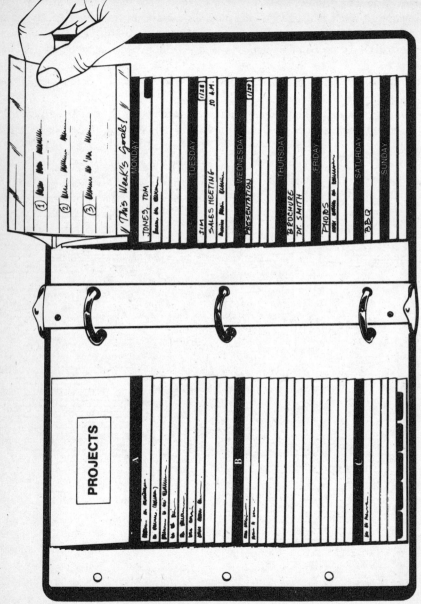

The Creative Organizer from Scan/Plan, Inc.

Scan/Plan uses standard 3″ by 5″ index cards. You can list a task on each card and file it under the corresponding day. Instead of rewriting your list, you simply move the cards forward when necessary. It's a flexible system that lets you use pieces of paper (the cards) but keeps them in one place.

What's important is not the uniqueness of the features in any of these planners, but whether or not they will actually help you. During one of my seminars, a woman told me that she had spent $150 on a planner and that she still wasn't organized. She felt she was a lost cause and would never be able to get organized. After all, if a $150 organizer couldn't organize her, what would? In fact, the problem wasn't that she couldn't get organized, but that she had bought the wrong planner. The sections in her expensive planner didn't have anything to do with her business, and the way the pages were laid out inside didn't suit the way she liked to record information.

When buying a predesigned organizer, find one that fits your needs, instead of attempting to adapt to it. Here are a few tips for selecting the right planner for you.

- Where will you keep this planner—in your briefcase, suit pocket, or purse? Select the appropriate size.
- Is the planner flexible enough for your needs?
- Are there too many sections that don't apply to you? (You *can* take them out, but why pay for something you don't need?)
- Are the "to do" sheets designed the way you would use them? For instance, are tasks separate from calls?
- Is there enough room to write on the monthly calendar and on the other sheets within each section?
- Does it look professional? If you want to project a certain image, a vinyl-bound planner may appear cheap, whereas a leather one would be more appropriate.

Know exactly why you are buying a planner before you buy it. One of my clients showed me a dozen planners she had bought with the intention of getting organized, but none of them helped. After we sat down and spent some time defining her needs, we were able to choose a commercially available planner that worked for her.

Feel free to tailor a predesigned planner to meet your needs. Experiment with sections you add yourself, and take out (or relabel) any sections that aren't appropriate for you (see Chapter 6). Few calendar companies include a section for personal tasks on their "to do" sheets. If your preprinted planner doesn't have a personal section, add one.

Some people worry that their planner won't look professional by the time they have finished customizing it, but in my view this hardly matters. A polished organizer that doesn't help you is useless. Again, it depends on your type of business. The important thing is to find or design a planner that works for you and then stick with it.

USING TICKLER FILES TO PLAN

If you find "to do" lists frustrating, or if you prefer to work with actual papers instead of lists, another personal planning option is a tickler file system, so named because your files are designed to "tickle" you when it is time to accomplish certain tasks. A tickler file system keeps your current papers organized and easily accessible. This is the approach I recommend to people who stuff papers in their planner (a bad idea, in that it prevents you from using your planner effectively and your papers can get lost or ruined).

Tickler file systems only work if you refer to them daily. I recommend using a "to do" list over a tickler system or in conjunction with a tickler system because this gives you greater control over the tasks that need your immediate attention. Also, if you choose this approach, your "to do" lists will reflect what papers are in your tickler files. However, I realize not everyone likes "to do" lists, and a tickler file system is better than nothing.

Before I describe them to you, it's only fair that I confess I am not fond of using tickler file systems in place of a "to do" list. A tickler file system is not as precise as a "to do" list; it's easier to ignore, it makes long-term planning difficult, and it increases the time it takes to retrieve papers because you have several places to look for any one document.

There are four basic approaches to tickler files. You can use either hanging files, a tickler book, an accordion file, or index cards. How you organize your tickler files depends on how you like to work.

The next chapter, "Stop Stacking and Start Filing," discusses various types of file folders and filing systems in detail. For now, concentrate on finding a basic organizing system that will work for you.

■ Tickler File System 1

Here is a step-by-step guide to setting up a tickler file system based on the days of the week.

1. *Find a place to store your tickler file folders.* In that they are current files—that is, you will be referring to them often—you need to keep them easily accessible. Either store them in your desk file drawer or in a vertical file holder on a surface near your desk (see Chapter 5).

2. *Label a hanging folder Weekly Activity.* Within this folder, place interior folders for each day of the week you work. For example, if you usually work Monday through Saturday, label six folders.

3. *Into these folders, put the papers you will be working on for the week.* In order to do this, you need to determine which projects are most urgent and when you are most likely to handle them.

4. *At the beginning of each day, look at that day's folder.* Work on those papers all day. If you don't get everything done, move the papers you haven't worked on into another day's folder.

With this system, you keep moving papers forward into the folders for upcoming days of the week until each task is accomplished. For long-term planning, add a folder labeled Future Tasks or Future Projects.

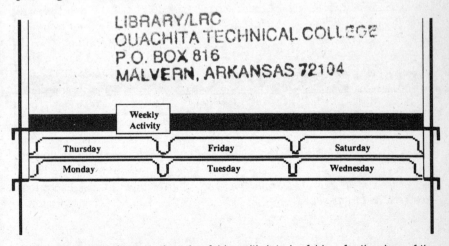

Tickler file system 1 uses a hanging folder with interior folders for the days of the week you work.

■ Tickler File System 2

Another approach to tickler file folders organizes your papers not by days of the week but according to their relative importance.

1. *Find an accessible place to store your tickler file folders.*
2. *Label a hanging file This Week.*
3. *Insert three interior files.* Label these files Hot, Important, and To Do.
4. *File the papers for your current projects in the interior files.* Put your most urgent projects in the Hot file folder, work that needs to be done soon in the Important folder, and tasks that need to be taken care of eventually in the To Do folder.
5. *Go through the Hot file every day, and look through the other files at least once a week.* With this system, papers for a project stay in the same file until you take care of the matter or until its status changes.

A variation on this system is to label a hanging file Hot Projects (instead of This Week), and to use interior folders for each project you need to look at every day.

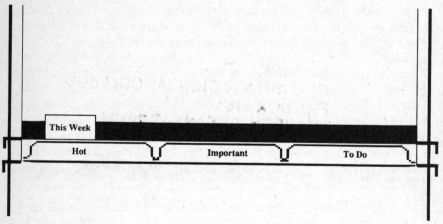

Tickler file system 2 uses a hanging folder with interior folders labeled according to your level of urgency.

It's important to go through these files regularly, in that tasks change in their level of importance. For example, a task that is only "to do" one week may become urgent the next week. You don't want to ignore projects in the last folder. For long-term planning, add a folder labeled Future Projects or Future Tasks.

■ Tickler File System 3

A more involved tickler file system allows you to plan for each day of the month and for upcoming months, just as you would with a planning note-book.

1. *Set up a vertical file holder in an accessible place.*
2. *Label a box-bottom hanging folder To Do.*
3. *Inside the box-bottom folder, place interior folders for each day of the month.* These files will always be used for the current month, so label them only with numbers, not with the name of the month. On April 12, for example, you would look inside the "12" folder.
4. *Label another box-bottom folder Upcoming Months.* Inside, put file folders labeled with the names of all of the months of the year.
5. *File papers that need your immediate attention in the To Do hanging folder under the appropriate date for the current month.*
6. *File papers that need your attention in the months ahead in the Upcoming Months hanging folder under the appropriate months.* Write the exact date that you will need to act on a piece of paper in its top right-hand corner.
7. *At the end of each day, move papers ahead.* If you didn't get everything done on a particular day, move the papers to another day (or month) when you will be able to handle them.
8. *At the end of each month, move papers ahead.* When a new month begins, take all papers out of the Upcoming Months file for that month and sort them into your daily "to do" folders. This will be easier to do if you were good about writing the action date in the upper corner of each paper.

With this system, you must continually rotate papers through your files, adding new projects, moving ahead any "to do" tasks that didn't get done, and cycling in projects that were filed under upcoming months.

To Do

28	29	30
25	26	27
22	23	24
19	20	21
16	17	18
13	14	15
10	11	12
7	8	9
4	5	6
1	2	3

Tickler file system 3 uses a box-bottom file with interior folders for all of the days of the month.

■ **Tickler File System 4**

This system requires an expanding "accordion" file. There are two types of expanding files: those with dividers and those without. Use the type with dividers.

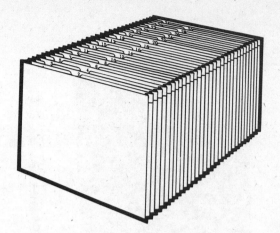

A prelabeled accordion file can be used with tickler file system 4. (Courtesy of Globe-Weis)

1. *Set up your expanding file in an accessible place.*
2. *Label the tabs on the dividers from 1 to 31 for the days of the month.*
Some expanding folders can be bought prelabeled. This folder will always be used for the current month, so it isn't necessary to add the name of the month. You will not need interior folders because you'll simply be putting papers into the pocket behind each tab.
3. *File papers that require action under the appropriate day of the month.* For example, work you need to do on the twelfth should be filed behind tab 12.
4. *Move your papers forward at the end of each day.* If a task hasn't been completed, move it ahead to the next day's compartment or to a day when you will be able to get the job done. A section for Future Projects will give you a place to store papers you'll need to refer to in the future.

■ **Tickler File System 5**

This system is much like the accordion folder system, except that you use a notebook instead of a folder. A tickler notebook comes prelabeled with dividers numbered 1 through 31. You don't need interior folders; instead, you just file your papers behind the appropriate tabs. An added benefit is that a tickler notebook also includes dividers for the twelve months of the year, enabling you to do your long-term planning alongside your short-term planning.

A tickler file notebook can be used in place of hanging files. (Courtesy of Smead)

■ Tickler File System 6

This system keeps you organized by means of index cards. You keep reminders on index cards, but file your actual paperwork elsewhere.

Index cards work well for people who like to write down reminders to themselves on pieces of paper. You can still write notes to yourself, but now you'll have a way to keep them absolutely organized.

1. *Get a small file box.*
2. *Insert cardboard dividers preprinted with the numbers 1 through 31.* These will correspond to the days of the current month.
3. *Insert cardboard dividers preprinted with all of the months of the year.* Place these behind the numbered dividers.
4. *Write your "to do" tasks on index cards.* Include a card for all current projects that need attention. When you think of something you must do, make a note of it on an index card.
5. *At the end of the day, move the cards ahead.* If any task hasn't been com-

pleted, move its card ahead to the next day or to a day (or month) when you will be able to complete it.

6. *At the end of the month, move the next month's cards forward.* Reminders for the next month are cycled in as each month is completed.

QUICK TIP FOR HOME OFFICE PROFESSIONALS

Remember to keep your momentum going. It's important to keep up with your filing every week. On your calendar, write "day to file" to remind you to file.

USING YOUR NEW PERSONAL PLANNING SYSTEM

Studies show that a new habit usually takes twenty-one days to take hold, so you can expect that it will take you about three weeks to get used to your new personal planning system. Even if you slip up, that's okay. Simply go back to your new and improved system and work to continually maintain it. After twenty-one days, it should become second nature. This can happen sooner, depending upon your level of desire.

One thing is certain: you won't use your personal planning system if you can't find it. Keep your planner or your tickler files where you can see them.

Jill, an attorney, was disciplined about filling in the "to do" sheets in her planner, but during the day she kept misplacing her planner and failing to check her list. She had no trouble, however, finding her billing notebook. When a client called, she would grab the notebook and record the call so that she could bill the client later. After we designated a certain spot in her office for both her billing notebook and her daily planner, she used her "to do" list more effectively.

Using a planner, "to do" list, and follow-up system will help you take control of your time and will take you quickly to the papers you need. In the next chapter, you'll learn how to get rid of the stacks of paper on your desk and to overcome the fear of filing.

8

STOP STACKING
AND START FILING

By now you've set up the perfect office. You have a workspace that meets your needs, you've cleaned out your desk, and you have stacking bins to organize your paperwork. However, so far you haven't put this model office to work. It's time to develop a system for handling and storing the papers you are currently working on.

WORKING STYLES

Everyone works in a different way and has different organizational needs. The techniques I suggest to one client may not work for another. The first step to knowing which organizational systems will make you more efficient is recognizing your own particular working style.

I've found that most people fall into one of the following five categories:

1. People who like to keep everything in sight. For you, out of sight is out of mind. You will lay papers out on your desk or even on the floor to remind you of what needs to be done. You've probably always functioned amidst clutter and have never felt it was a problem. The right organizational systems for you will enable you to put away your papers but still keep them at hand and on your mind. You will find that instead of keeping an entire project in view, it's sufficient to keep only a reminder (your "to do" list) in view.

2. People who like to stuff everything in drawers. You are so determined to give your home office an organized look you hide things in drawers or closets without taking the time to process them first. You've got the surfaces under control, which has a calming effect on you, but actually you're generating as much clutter as the person who leaves everything on top of a desk or on the floor. You need organizational systems that will enable you to quickly put things in their proper places. This will keep your surfaces neat and will help keep you from wasting time looking for things.

3. Perfectionists. You love details and are concerned about doing things perfectly, no matter how long it takes. You have high standards of excellence. You think you're organized because the items on your desk are perfectly aligned and everything has been typed to perfection. The right organizational systems for you will help you keep your paperwork extremely organized, but with a minimum of obsessing. This will help you focus on the big picture—what you are and are not accomplishing—instead of the insignificant details.

4. People who jump from task to task. You have an active mind and have difficulty concentrating on just one thing at a time. You're constantly jumping from project to project without finishing one of them. For example, you make a phone call, then start to write yourself a note about it, but then notice yesterday's mail and start to open it, which reminds you that you'd like a cup of coffee . . . and so on. The right organizational systems for you will help you stay focused on one task at a time so that your productivity increases.

5. People who can't make up their minds. You hate making decisions because in every situation you see so many possibilities. It's difficult to make decisions because so many approaches have merit. You're afraid that by committing yourself to one course of action you may be closing off another avenue that might be better. You need organizational systems that will help you keep moving papers forward, even if you put off making decisions about them.

Tina and Mitch, husband and wife, were sales reps for a line of costume jewelry. Tina took care of the paperwork (invoices, correspondence, sales reports) and Mitch concentrated on selling (appointments, promotion, following up on leads). Their skills complemented each other beautifully *except* in their office, where their different approaches created chaos.

Tina was a drawer-stuffer, but Mitch liked to leave everything in front of him. Not only were they getting in each other's way, but between the two of them they had managed to clutter up their entire office.

To get Tina and Mitch out of their mess, we set up some office systems that would work for both of them. Stacking bins appealed to Tina because they provided a place to put things, and they were also okay with Mitch, in that he could see at a glance what was where. We brought in a file cart for paperwork, and they rolled it back and forth between the two of them as needed. We labeled absolutely everything so that there would be no question about where items should be stored. We also set up some filing systems to ensure that if one of them filed something, the other would be able to find it. After Tina and Mitch dug themselves out of the mess they had created, they had no trouble staying organized. If they started to slip up, there was already a system in place to get them back on track.

QUICK TIP FOR HOME OFFICE PROFESSIONALS

Don't choose an organizational system you don't like. There's no point trying to implement an approach that doesn't suit your working style. If a particular approach doesn't appeal to you, find an alternative that does. There's always another way to get organized.

PAPER, PAPER EVERYWHERE

When you work in a home office, the only limit on the number of piles of paper you create is the space available in the rooms of your home—and possibly a garage.

Melinda, a graphics designer, told the audience at one of my seminars that she had so many stacks of paper she started filling cardboard boxes with pile after pile of papers. When she ran out of boxes, she used her wastebasket. Finally she put the boxes and the wastebasket outside the door of her office, preparing to store her papers in the basement. When she came home from an appointment, she discovered that the housekeeper had thrown everything away, thinking it was trash—which, after all, was just what Melinda's papers had looked like. At that moment, Melinda knew she could no longer put off getting organized. People keep stacks of paper spread throughout their office and home for a variety of reasons.

- They haven't made a decision about each piece of paper.
- They want to remind themselves of tasks they need to accomplish.
- They're afraid of filing a piece of paper and never seeing it again.
- They don't have specific places to put their papers.
- They want to keep a document around "just in case."

The solution is to follow the rule "move it forward." Do something to move each piece of paper forward from the minute it comes into your office. You don't have to make final decisions about what action to take, but you do need to decide what you are going to do with the paper involved. First sort, then file your papers until you need them again.

At first it will feel different to do something with each piece of paper instead of just setting it aside. Once you get into this habit, however, you will no longer have stacks of paper in your office.

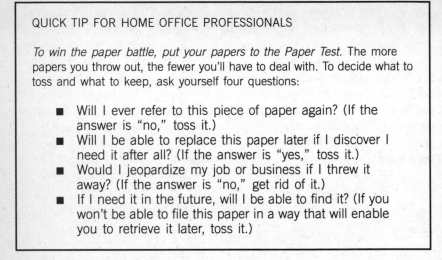

QUICK TIP FOR HOME OFFICE PROFESSIONALS

To win the paper battle, put your papers to the Paper Test. The more papers you throw out, the fewer you'll have to deal with. To decide what to toss and what to keep, ask yourself four questions:

- Will I ever refer to this piece of paper again? (If the answer is "no," toss it.)
- Will I be able to replace this paper later if I discover I need it after all? (If the answer is "yes," toss it.)
- Would I jeopardize my job or business if I threw it away? (If the answer is "no," get rid of it.)
- If I need it in the future, will I be able to find it? (If you won't be able to file this paper in a way that will enable you to retrieve it later, toss it.)

SORTING YOUR PAPERS

The task you are about to embark on will take time, so make sure you block out at least three hours. The following is a step-by-step plan to sorting all of the papers in your office:

1. Gather all of the work-related papers in your office and throughout your home and put the stacks in one area.
2. Sort these papers into the following five piles. Don't stop to read each piece of paper; at this point, you're only sorting.

- *To do.* These papers need immediate attention. Keep them on your desk for now.
- *To file.* These papers need to be stored in your filing cabinet. Put them in your "to file" stacking bin for the time being.
- *To read.* This may include magazines, newspapers, or any other papers you want to read at a later date. These go in your "to read" stacking bin.
- *To sort.* These are papers you need to look at more closely after you have set up a current file system (described in this

chapter). Keep them on your desk for now, separate from your "to do" stack.

■ *To toss.* Throw out any papers you will never refer to again, including junk mail.

3. Go back to your "to do" pile. As you look at each piece of paper, record any action you need to take on the "to do" list in your personal planner. (If you chose another personal organizing system from Chapter 7, use that.) After you've made a note on your "to do" list, these papers should be filed in your current file system, which you are about to create. Put your "to do" stack aside for now.

Before you actually start filing any of this paperwork, you need to have a basic understanding of filing principles, so let's take a break from office cleaning and move to filing basics.

QUICK TIP FOR HOME OFFICE PROFESSIONALS

Keep your personal and business papers separate. Otherwise, you end up constantly looking through your business files to find the personal files you need. Also, if your spouse handles the personal files, he or she will constantly be in your office looking for them. The ideal approach is to buy a two-drawer filing cabinet to use for personal papers. If that's not possible, devote one full drawer of your filing cabinet to personal papers only. If you come across stock certificates, bonds, or the title to your car as you're going through your papers, set them aside until you can put them in your safe deposit box. Put information about your credit cards—including the card number and the number to call if your card is lost or stolen—in a personal file labeled Important Numbers.

TYPES OF FILES

There are three types of files: current, reference, and historical. The only similarity between the three is that they are all papers you might like to see again. Keeping them separate makes it easier for you to get your hands on whatever paper you need when you need it.

- *Current files* contain papers that currently need your attention. This could include a letter that needs your response, a report to write, or papers from a project in progress. Current files need to be kept at your fingertips in your desk drawer file, your vertical file, or the rolling file cart mentioned in Chapter 5.
- *Reference files* are those you don't use often, but still need to have accessible. They include any information you may need at a later date, but not on a daily basis. Examples include papers related to clients, past reports you have completed, letters you have sent, and relevant articles from magazines. Reference files belong in your office in a filing cabinet (or similar alternative).
- *Historical files* are files you seldom, if ever, refer to, but need to keep for legal reasons. Examples include past tax returns, inactive client files, paid invoices, or any files over three years old. Historical files should be taken out of your filing cabinet and stored away safely in a sturdy box labeled with the contents and date.

THE P-A-P-E-R SYSTEM

You have five options when it comes to dealing with paper.

Put it in a stacking bin.
Act on it.
Put it in a file.
Enter it on your "to do" list and file it.
Rid yourself of it.

Put it in a stacking bin. Stacking bins are a temporary place to put papers you want to read or file. These papers do not require immediate action. Before you put a piece of paper in your "to file" bin, write in the upper right-hand corner the name of the reference file where it should go.

Act on it. Acting on a piece of paper means you take action on it at that moment. That could include sending immediate payment to someone or writing a response on someone's note and sending it back (a fast alternative to writing a new letter).

Put it in a file. If you have the time, immediately put papers in the appropriate reference files.

Enter it on your list and file it. For papers that require action soon, make a note of what needs to be done on your "to do" list on the day you are going to take action. Then file the paper in the appropriate current file until you are ready to work on it. If you will need the paper as a backup later but don't need it to work on the project, put it in your reference files. Some current papers may not require a note on your "to do" list because they go with information you already have. Put a document like this immediately in the correct current file.

Rid yourself of it. This means either recycle it or trash it.

The saying "handle paper once" has been used for years. It sounds efficient, but it is frequently not possible. Instead, do something with each piece of paper to move it forward. For example, suppose you receive a bill from your printer. You handle it the first time when you open it, but it's not bill-paying time yet. So you file the paper in your "bills to pay" file. When you pay the bills, you'll handle it again. There is absolutely nothing wrong with handling paper this way. What you want to avoid is picking up a piece of paper, wondering what to do with it, then putting it back in a stack on your desk. When this happens, you haven't done anything to move things forward.

HANGING FILE FOLDERS

There are many types of hanging file folders.

- Cardboard or plastic
- Plain or reinforced (to ensure the folder doesn't separate from the metal hanging rod)
- Box-bottom (wide bottom, no sides)
- Hanging box (wide bottom, half sides)
- Two-inch, three-inch, and four-inch widths
- Letter size or legal size
- With or without plastic sleeves for storing computer disks

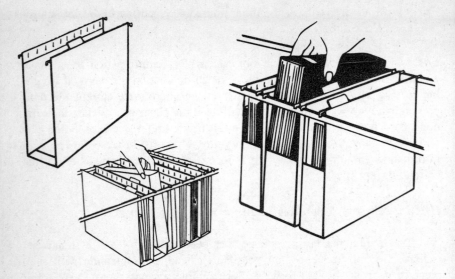

Box-bottom folders (left) *have a wide bottom and can accommodate thick files, notebooks, or several interior folders. Hanging box files* (right) *have sides to keep papers from falling out. (Courtesy of Esselte Pendaflex Corporation)*

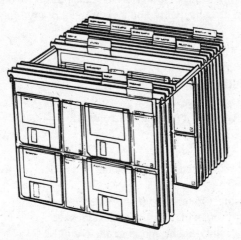

Hanging folders with plastic sleeves allow you to file computer disks with the papers that go with them. (Courtesy of Ring King Visibles, Inc.)

The amount of papers you'll be storing in a hanging folder determines which type to use. Hanging folders are meant to be a guide, not to be taken in and out of your filing cabinet or vertical file holder.

INTERIOR FILE FOLDERS

Inside your hanging folders you'll be placing interior file folders. These are meant to be taken in and out of your filing cabinet. There is a large assortment of these, too.

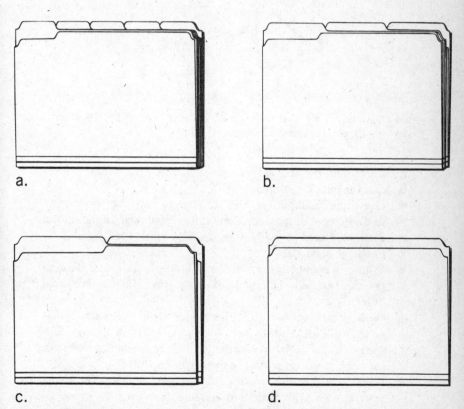

a.   b.

c.   d.

Interior file folders are available in (a) one-fifth, (b) one-third, (c) one-half, or (d) straight cut. Which you choose depends on the number of tabs you need to be able to see at once.

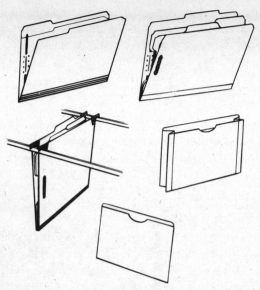

Interior file folders come in a wide variety of types to suit various filing needs. (Courtesy of Esselte Pendaflex Corporation)

- Cardboard, pressboard, or plastic.
- Plain manila or colored.
- One-fifth, one-third, one-half, or straight cut. The "cut" refers to the number of tabs there are on the upper edge of the folder.
- Plain or scored at the bottom (to allow for expansion).
- Letter or legal size.
- With or without fasteners inside to hold papers secure. Fasteners are especially helpful in keeping papers in chronological order.
- With or without sides. A file folder sealed on each end is called a file jacket. File jackets keep papers or disks from falling out of the folder. Available in plain or expanding versions, they are ideal for holding papers you need to take with you.
- Partition folders use interior fasteners and divide a file folder into sections, with cardboard dividers. They may be stored inside hanging folders or hung on file rods.

In addition, there are other products made to be used with file folders, such as self-adhesive pockets that attach inside file folders to hold computer disks or small papers.

LABELING HANGING FOLDERS

Take the time to carefully label your hanging folders. This will save you time later when you're looking through your files. For hanging folders, you can use either of the following:

- Plastic tabs (clear or colored), with white inserts you write on
- Tabs you write directly on, then attach to your folders

The big question with hanging folders is whether to put the plastic tab with the label on the front or the back of the folder. This is entirely a matter of preference. I don't care which approach you choose, but I do recommend that you be consistent. That way you won't put papers in the wrong folders because you pushed a folder back when you should have pulled it forward.

LABELING INTERIOR FILE FOLDERS

Although it takes an extra minute, it's important to label your interior folders as well because they won't be inside hanging folders when you're using them. Labeling makes refiling easier, especially after you've taken out several files. For interior folders, you can use any of the following:

- Self-adhesive file folder labels that you write on
- Electronic labeler
- Your own handwriting

Avoid the old-fashioned gummed labels that need to be moistened before use; they don't stay attached very well. If you're constantly ruining file tabs, you can put clear adhesive protectors (available at an office supply store) over your file labels to protect them.

An electronic labeler will generate typed, adhesive-backed labels with which to label many things in your home office, including interior file folders. (Courtesy of Kroy Inc.)

SETTING UP YOUR CURRENT FILE SYSTEM

In a desk drawer file, vertical file holder, or file cart (see Chapter 5), you now want to organize the papers on which you are currently working. If you set up a tickler file system (see Chapter 7), use it in conjunction with your current files. If you have a hanging file system, use hanging folders. If you're using a vertical file holder that accommodates only interior files, skip the following steps for hanging folders.

1. Start by labeling a hanging folder Action.
2. Inside this hanging folder, put two interior folders labeled To Do and Pending. (You may prefer Follow-Up instead of Pending.) If you write letters to prospective clients and are waiting to hear from them, you could add another folder labeled Prospects.
3. Label another hanging folder Bills. Stagger the plastic tabs on your hanging folders so that you can read them.
4. Inside this hanging folder, place an interior folder labeled Bills to Pay. If you pay bills twice a month, instead of using Bills to Pay, use two folders labeled 1 and 15. If you charge any business purchases, add another interior folder labeled Charges. Stagger the tabs on the interior folders (left, middle, right) so that you can read them.

5. Label another hanging folder Projects. Inside put a separate interior folder for each of your current projects.

6. Add any other categories you may need, based on the papers in your "to do" stack. For example, you might need a hanging folder labeled Orders, with interior folders labeled Orders to Place and Pending Orders. Or you might need a hanging folder labeled Letters, with interior folders labeled Letters to Write and Waiting for Response. If you have staff working for you, you might create a Staff hanging folder and put in it an interior folder for each staff member.

Avoid labeling any files Miscellaneous. That's an open invitation to keep papers you will probably never refer to again, or at least won't be able to find.

To be extra organized, use a different color for each group of hanging and interior files. For example, all of your interior folders under Bills to Pay could be green.

USING YOUR CURRENT FILE SYSTEM

Now you're ready to file your "to do" stack. This is the point at which some of you will learn that out of sight does *not* have to mean out of mind.

Before you file anything in your current files, remember to make a note of any action necessary on your "to do" list. This will wean you away from the habit of keeping papers on your desk in order to remind you to take care of them. Next to the notation on your list, you could put the name of the file in which you place the related papers. This way your "to do" list will take you directly to the correct papers.

Use the hanging folders and/or interior folders you just set up to file your "to do" papers. When you come across papers that don't fit into an existing category, set them aside until you're finished filing the rest. Then go back and decide if you should start a new folder for these papers in your current files, if they could possibly go in your reference files, or if you can toss them.

1. In the To Do folder, put the papers that need immediate action.

2. The Pending (or Follow-Up) interior folder is for papers that need some type of response from someone else or some type of action from you at a later date. For example, if you sent a letter to someone and are waiting to hear back from that person, keep the letter in your Pending file. You could also keep in this file information about a seminar you will be attending in a few weeks.

3. File your bills under either Bills or 1 and 15, depending on how many folders you created for bills. Put charge receipts in your Charges folder. (Later you can compare them against your bill.)

4. Group any paperwork about current projects in the Projects hanging folder in the appropriate interior files. Each project should have its own interior folder.

Exception 1 is any project that has generated only one or two pieces of paper. Projects with little paperwork can be grouped together in an interior folder labeled Projects.

Exception 2 is any project that has generated a lot of paper. If an interior folder is more than an inch thick, it deserves its own hanging folder, labeled with the name of the project, and filled with separate interior folders corresponding to various aspects of the project.

After you have sorted your "to do" pile, go back to your "to sort" pile and decide what to do with those papers. If any of them fall into the "to do" category, you now know what to do with them.

When you are finished, there shouldn't be any stacks of paper left on your desk. All of your papers should have been stored in your current files, placed in stacking bins, or thrown away. Here are some examples of how to process papers by using your "to do" list.

Piece of Paper	**"To Do" List**
A letter from a client requesting information.	Write down, "Send information to XYZ."
A brochure describing a seminar you want to attend.	Write down, "Send registration form and check for seminar."
A brochure describing a conference you might want to attend.	On the "to do" sheet for the appropriate day, make a note of the deadline for registration.

Notes from a recent conversation with a client.	Transfer any items from your action box to your "to do" list, then put the notes in your "to file" stacking bin.
Your phone bill.	Check the payment due date. Write down "pay phone bill" a week ahead of that date to avoid late charges.

QUICK TIP FOR HOME OFFICE PROFESSIONALS

Never store papers flat. Papers are easier to find when they are stored vertically in files, rather than horizontally in piles. The only time your papers should be stored horizontally is when you place them in stacking bins, and this is only on a temporary basis. Eventually the papers in the bins will be stored vertically or thrown away.

CLEARING OUT YOUR CURRENT FILES

Current files are for papers that need action. Once no further action is required, papers should go in reference files (see Chapter 9) or be tossed. Go through your current files at least once a week to get rid of papers that don't belong there. You need to keep papers continuously flowing through your current files. If you don't, your current files will start to fill up with reference files, which will make it more difficult to find the papers you need right away. It also makes it more difficult to focus on the tasks that need immediate attention.

Getting rid of stacks of paper in your office is the first phase of paper control. In the next chapter, you'll learn how to make your reference files manageable.

9

HOME OFFICE
FILING SYSTEMS

No matter what size your home office is, you will need to have some type of filing system that goes beyond the current-file system described in Chapter 8. Whether you need several filing cabinets or just a milk crate to hold your files, the key is to be able to quickly find the papers you need.

I've seen filing cabinets used for all sorts of things. Some people use them for all three types of files: current, reference, and historical (see Types of Files, pages 113–14). Some people use them to store office supplies. Many people, when they run out of room, go out and buy more filing cabinets, or filing crates, or file carts. However, before you invest in more filing cabinets, why not clean out the files you already have?

Now that you've taken all of the unnecessary items out of your office and removed all of the unnecessary things from your desktop, it's time to purge your files.

TWO TYPES OF REFERENCE FILES: CURRENT AND OLDER

In Chapter 8, you were given procedures for setting up current files for papers you are currently working on. Now you will turn your attention to papers that you may want to look at again someday, but that you don't need to have at your fingertips.

You already know from Chapter 8 that these remaining files will fall into two categories: reference files (keep accessible) and historical files (store where you'll be able to find them if necessary). Most home office professionals find it useful to subdivide their reference files into two subcategories, *current reference* and *older reference*.

Current reference files are different from current files because they are used often, but not on a daily basis. Examples of current reference files include the following:

- Backup documents for current projects
- Client files
- Mailing lists
- Sales materials

Older reference files contain papers from past projects or events. You may refer to these files once or twice a month. Examples of older reference files include the following:

- Articles from magazines
- Competitive information
- Notes from a seminar you attended
- Past client information

As you sort the remaining papers in your office, you will need to start thinking in terms of four file categories.

1. Current
2. Current reference
3. Older reference
4. Historical

Once you get in the habit of thinking this way, all of your filing decisions become much easier.

PURGING YOUR FILES

You may have stacked your paperwork in your "to file" stacking bin, or you may have files already in filing cabinets. If they're in your cabinets, go through them one drawer at a time.

If you're a pack rat, you may be faced with an overwhelming number of files. Going through your files and keeping only the ones you need may seem to be an impossible task. Don't be surprised if your office looks worse during this sorting process than it did when you started. Keep in mind that this disaster is only temporary, and that when you're finished your office will look much better than it did originally. Still, be prepared for unsolicited advice from family members and friends while you are elbow deep in files.

Throughout the sorting process, don't stop to read every paper. Just sort. It's important to make a quick decision about each file. Here is a step-by-step guide to purging your files:

1. *Sort all your paperwork into four piles: "current reference," "older reference," "historical," and "to sort."* Your current files and personal papers should all have been taken care of (see Chapter 8). Have a trash can nearby for papers to toss.

2. *First deal with your historical files.* Put them in sturdy boxes with a lid. Then label them with the date and the contents. Store these files in a closet, preferably in your office, otherwise on pallets in your garage, basement, or attic. If storage space is limited, you could take them to be microfilmed or store them off-site in a storage unit. Before you spend the money on these alternatives, make sure the information you are keeping is worth saving. The point is to keep your historical files out of the mainstream of your home office.

3. *Now turn your attention to your pile of current reference files.* For the next level of organizing, start grouping similar current reference files together. For example, your client files should all be together.

4. *Place your current reference files in the top drawer of your filing cabinet, or the part of the cabinet that is most accessible.* Later on you will learn more about various filing systems, but for now all you need to do is put your current reference files in your cabinet.

5. *Organize your older reference files into groups, as you did with your current reference files.*

6. *Put your older reference files in the bottom drawer of your filing cabinet, or the part of the cabinet that is least accessible.*

7. *Before you go any further, go through each file and take out papers you no longer need.* Remember the Paper Test on page 112. Avoid the tendency to jump from drawer to drawer. Start with one drawer and work on it until you're finished. As you go through each drawer, you will find files that belong elsewhere. Either keep them in a stack on the floor until you get to them, or go ahead and place them in the correct drawers.

8. *By now you should have taken care of all of your historical, current reference, and older reference files, as well as any current files or personal papers that might have sneaked into this process.* Look at your "to sort" pile last and decide which category is appropriate for each file. You may be surprised to find, as you look through this pile, that most of the items will be strong candidates for the trash.

QUICK TIP FOR HOME OFFICE PROFESSIONALS

Give your files names that will immediately come to mind when you need a piece of paper. Use word association. There is no general guide to naming files, in that this is a very individual matter. What works for you may not work for another person. The only filing system that will work for you is one that is customized to meet your needs. In a home office, you'll probably be the only one using the files, so it doesn't matter if the names mean nothing to anyone else. However, if anyone else will be using your files, explain your system to him or her.

FILING 101

Before you set up filing systems within your filing cabinet, review the following filing basics:

1. Make sure your filing cabinet has a frame for hanging folders inside. Always use hanging folders in your filing cabinet, and always use interior folders inside the hanging folders; hanging folders are not designed to be taken in and out of your cabinet regularly.

Some people just stuff their interior folders in their filing cabinet drawer, maybe with some cardboard dividers between them. This is a bad idea. It takes longer to find the file folder you need because it's difficult to read the labels on the tabs, the folders often slip down because they have little support, and you have a tendency to ruin folders and make the labels illegible because you're constantly pushing and pulling on them. When you use hanging folders, you pull on the hanging folder, not on the interior folder itself.

2. A topic doesn't really deserve its own interior folder until you have accumulated about eight pieces of paper for it. Until then, group related topics together in one interior folder. For example, suppose several people wrote to you inquiring about your services, and you answered each of them with a simple letter. Staple your responses to the original letters and file all of this correspondence together. If one person turns out to be serious about what you have to offer and you end up exchanging several letters, it's time to label a new interior folder with the name of that individual.

3. Use more than one interior folder within each hanging folder. You don't need a separate hanging folder for each project or client until the interior folder starts getting too full. Too many hanging folders means too many places to look for one piece of paper. They also take up more space in your filing cabinet.

4. Keep your folders up to half an inch thick (about fifty sheets). When they get thicker than that, divide the file folder into subcategories. For example, suppose you have a hanging folder labeled Projects, and inside there is an interior folder labeled Wilson Project that is getting too big. Divide the Wilson folder into interior folders for various aspects of the project. Then label a hanging folder Wilson Project and put the interior folders in it.

5. Create an index that lists all of your hanging and interior folders. This reduces the chance of your duplicating files. Also, when you need to find a piece of paper, the index will help you go to the right file. The best place to keep your index is in an interior folder labeled Index, inside a hanging folder with the same name and kept at the front of your filing cabinet.

A sample portion of your index might look like this.

FORMS (HANGING FOLDER)
  Client contact forms (interior folder)
  Order forms
  Project planner forms

6. Before you file a piece of paper, write in the top right-hand corner the name of the file where it belongs. Another option is to highlight a key word that corresponds to an existing file. If you need to create a file, write the new file name in the corner of the paper or attach a sticky note with the new file name written on it. (There are preprinted detachable notes available that have the word *file* on them.)

When you put the name of the correct files on your papers, the next time you take them out of your filing cabinet, you'll know exactly where they belong. You'll also save yourself the headache of creating new files unnecessarily because you weren't certain if an appropriate file already existed.

7. After putting the name of the file in the top right-hand corner, put a purge date at the top as well. This makes it easier to throw away papers you no longer need. Every time you take out a file, throw away any outdated papers. In addition, go through your filing cabinet at least every six months and get rid of papers you are no longer using.

8. Label the outside of each file drawer. That way you'll save time opening and closing drawers, looking for files.

9. Stagger the tabs. Do this on the interior folders within each hanging folder and on the hanging folders so that you can easily see each one.

10. If you're hard on interior folders . . . For example, if you take the same one out a lot, consider buying interior folders made of plastic that can withstand the wear and tear.

11. Avoid filing papers with paper clips attached. These bulk up your files. Even worse, they often catch on other papers and make it difficult to find the papers you need.

LETTER SIZE OR LEGAL SIZE?

I am often asked which size folder is better, letter size or legal size. Unless you are in the legal profession, most of your documents will probably be letter size, making legal-size folders unnecessary. Letter-size folders, in that they are smaller, also make a more efficient use of space.

If you inherited a legal-size filing cabinet, you don't have to use legal-size folders. Instead, buy a letter-size file frame, put it in the drawers, and hang letter-size hanging folders on it.

QUICK TIP FOR HOME OFFICE PROFESSIONALS

Keep your filing systems easy to use. If you choose a filing system that is too difficult to use, or if you get bogged down with details such as whether or not to type the labels on your file folders and whether or not to use color-coordinated tabs and folders, you'll end up never filing anything.

FINDING THE RIGHT FILING SYSTEM FOR YOU

There are three basic types of filing systems you can use with hanging and interior folders. You have the option of filing your papers according to one of the following systems:

- Alphabetically
- By category
- Numerically

The papers you are filing can be broken down into three categories.

1. By type (bills, letters, reports)
2. By name (corporation or individual)
3. By geographic location (city, state)

The key to filing is to make the system fit your needs and to make the retrieval of papers easy. Using color with any filing system makes it possible to file and retrieve papers more easily and more quickly.

ALPHABETICAL ORDER: WHAT COMES FIRST?

Whichever filing system you choose, you need to be familiar with the correct way to put files in alphabetical order. The following are some all-purpose rules for filing alphabetically:

1. File nothing before something. For example:

Jones, William
Jones, William A.
Jones, William C.

2. Spell out numbers to file them. For example, the numbers 1, 2, 3, 23, and 71 would be filed as follows:

one
seventy-one
three
twenty-three
two

3. Put last names before first names. For example:

Brown, J. (not J. Brown)
White, L. (not L. White)

4. Completely spell out company names and then file them by the entire name. For example, use Madison Franklin Enterprises, not Enterprises, Madison Franklin, or Franklin Enterprises, Madison.
5. Disregard articles (a, the) when filing. For example, *The Book of Lists* should be filed under *B*.

ALPHABETICAL FILING SYSTEMS

The alphabetical filing system is ideal for the following types of files:

■ Clients
■ Company information
■ Research information

This is the most basic filing system, and it is often used in home offices. It works well when it is applied to the right types of papers and when one main subject will be placed in a file drawer.

John, a financial planner, filed all of his papers alphabetically. This worked well for filing his client information, but fell apart with other topics. As his files began to grow, related information ended up being stored in different drawers of his filing cabinet, and he discovered he was spending too much time searching for the files he needed. John's files looked something like this.

Bane, William [client]
Bills to pay [current]
Boy Scouts [information about his son's troop]
Brian [his son]
Brown, John [another client]
Budget [current]
Budget [from three years ago]

Part of John's problem was that he was stuffing interior folders into his filing cabinet without using hanging folders. This contributed to the lack of organization in his office and the amount of time he was wasting looking for files. In addition, there were several other things wrong with his system.

■ Current files were mixed up with reference files.
■ Personal and business papers were stored together.
■ Client files were mixed with other files.

The first thing John had to do was set up a separate location for his current files. Then he had to sort his papers as we just discussed, putting the historical files into storage, placing the personal papers in a separate drawer, and separating current reference files from older reference files. After investing in hanging file folders, John was ready to pick a better way to refile his paperwork.

■ Alphabetical Filing System 1

The following is a basic approach to alphabetical filing:

1. Label tabs on hanging folders with each letter of the alphabet. You'll probably want to stagger the tabs so that they are easier to read. Box-bottom hanging folders are useful for thick files.
2. Within the A hanging folder, place interior folders for subjects that begin with the letter A. Limit the interior folders to six per hanging folder.
3. If you have more interior folders to file under A, start another hanging folder for them. You can add another A tab, or skip adding any more tabs until you get to B.

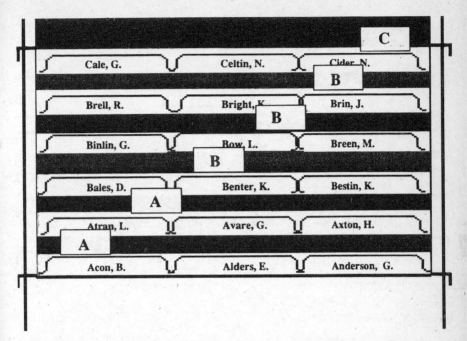

Alphabetical filing system 1: a basic approach to alphabetizing your files.

■ Alphabetical Filing System 2

This system adds a "catchall" file at the beginning of the files for each letter. Use these extra folders to hold papers that do not have their own files. When you have enough papers that are related to one another, start a file folder for these.

1. Set up your files as in Alphabetical Filing System 1.
2. Label an extra hanging folder for each letter of the alphabet.
3. Inside these hanging folders, add interior folders labeled with the corresponding letters of the alphabet.
4. Place these extra hanging folders at the beginning of the files for each letter of the alphabet.

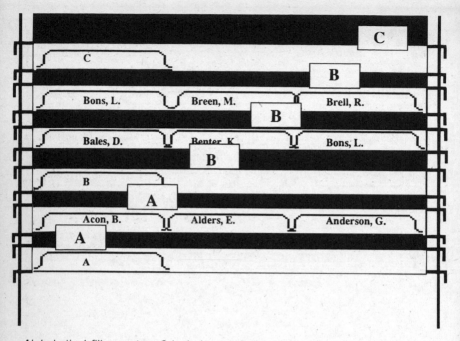

Alphabetical filing system 2 includes catchall hanging folders for each letter.

■ Alphabetical Filing System 3

I recommend that you avoid filing all types of papers together. However, old habits are sometimes difficult to break, and you may find it easier to group all of your paperwork together, no matter what the subject, and file your papers strictly alphabetically. If that's the case, you need to do the following:

1. Label a catchall hanging folder for each letter of the alphabet as in Alphabetical Filing System 2. Use this folder for papers that don't have their own files.
2. Behind these hanging folders, file your papers alphabetically. Group your papers together as much as possible, and label each hanging folder with a main category (for example, Accounts, Advertising, Articles). Inside, file subcategories in labeled interior files. Box-bottom hanging folders may be helpful.

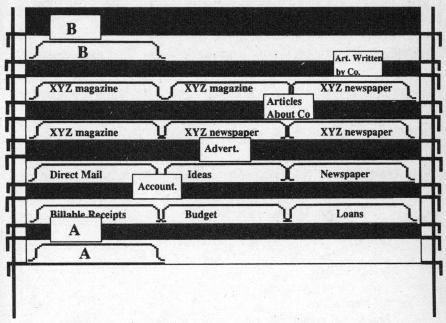

Alphabetical filing system 3 groups papers alphabetically by topic.

CATEGORICAL FILING SYSTEMS

The categorical filing system is ideal for the following types of files:

- Articles on specific topics
- Associations
- Forms
- Projects
- Receipts
- Sales sheets

With a categorical filing system, you group similar information. This system uses the principle of a main category and subcategories, with the hanging folder used for the main category and interior folders used for the subcategories. Filing by category has several advantages.

1. Related information is kept together.
2. You have fewer places to look for each piece of paper.

3. Files are in bite-size pieces.
4. You don't need to cross-reference your files because similar papers are already grouped together.

The following outline is an example of a categorical filing system:

ADVERTISING
   Direct Mail
   Newspaper
   Radio

ASSOCIATION (GIVE NAME)
   Correspondence
   Newsletters

FORMS
   Fax Cover Sheets
   Invoices
   Order Forms
   Prospect Sheets
   Standard Contract

MARKETING
   Clubs for Speeches
   Cold Calling
   Direct Mail

■ How to Set Up a Categorical Filing System

The basic approach to categorical filing is as follows:

1. Group your interior file folders together by main category.
2. Label a hanging folder with the name of each main category and place the interior folders inside in alphabetical order.
3. Place the hanging folders in your file drawer either in order of importance or alphabetically. The alphabetical approach is simplest, but it may be problematic for you if you'll constantly be reaching into the back of your file drawer for a folder that's filed under *V*.

With a categorical filing system, you file papers alphabetically within categories.

You could use a different colored tab for each overall category. This way, when you open your file drawer you'll easily see the separation of files by category.

NUMERICAL FILING SYSTEMS

The numerical filing system employs numbers instead of letters or words. This filing system is ideal for the following types of files:

- Confidential files
- Invoices
- Temporary files

The advantages of filing numerically are the following:

1. *Privacy.* If your office is also used as a guest room, your guests won't easily be able to tell what is inside each file folder. Unless you're familiar with the system, it would take awhile to find a particular folder.

2. *Speed.* When you need to find a piece of paper, you look at the numerical index and it will take you right to it. Numbers are easier to locate than names.

3. *Flexibility.* If you throw away the contents of a folder, you can still use the folder for a new subject. There's no need to relabel an interior folder. All you have to do is update your index.

The following outline is an example of a simple numerical filing system:

1. ADVERTISING
    A. Direct Mail
    B. Newspaper
    C. Radio
2. FINANCE
    A. CDs
    B. IRAs
    C. Money Markets

This is the least complicated numerical system you could use. Numbers don't work for everyone, but they are an option to consider.

■ How to Set Up a Numerical Filing System

The following is a basic approach to numerical filing:

1. Label each hanging folder with a consecutive number.

2. Write these numbers on an index.

3. Group your interior folders by category or subject.

4. Label the interior folders with the number of a hanging folder and place them inside the appropriate hanging folders.

5. After staggering the tabs on the interior folders, add a letter to each one (1A, 1B, 1C).

6. Enter an overall description of the contents of each folder on your index.

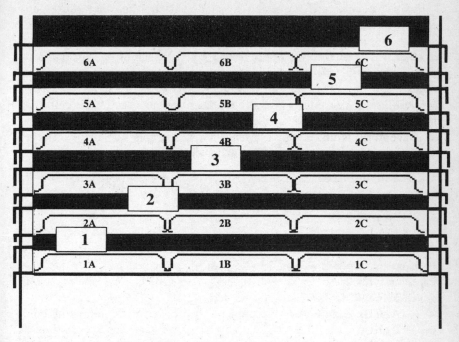

With a numerical filing system, each folder is given a number instead of a letter or word.

COLOR CODING YOUR FILES

Color coding may be used with any filing system. With the color-coding method, colors are used to visually separate letters, categories, or numbers.

You can use colored hanging folders, colored interior folders, and/or colored tabs on the hanging folders, depending on how involved you want to get. Within an alphabetically arranged file drawer, for example, the *A*'s could be red, the *B*'s yellow, and the *C*'s blue. With a categorical filing system, each category could be a different color. With a numerical system, numbers 1 through 25 could be one color, or the files that relate to one another could be one color.

Some home office professionals use different colored folders for different file drawers. Everything in the top drawer, for example, goes in a red folder. This makes refiling easier.

Some people feel it's easier to get organized when they use colors. Judy, the office manager of a four-person home office, had struggled with getting organized for years. She found the standard filing methods too rigid. For her, we devised a filing system and a daily planning system based on colors. The papers that needed her immediate attention were placed in red folders, and those that had to do with finances were in green. She had to keep track of the schedules of two bosses, and so gave each one a color. On her daily "to do" list, she highlighted the tasks in colors that corresponded to the appropriate folders. Less visually oriented people sometimes made remarks about Judy's "rainbow office," but the fact was, this system worked for her where others hadn't.

FILING IN BINDERS

Some people prefer to file their papers in notebooks or binders instead of file folders. One of my clients, who worked in finance, had over the years built up a bookcase filled with binders that were clearly labeled and in which he could find anything he needed.

If you have more shelf space than file space, try using three-ring binders to free up your filing cabinet. This way you can keep papers such as warranty information on your shelf instead of having them take up space in your file drawers.

Binders will work well if you do the following:

1. Clearly label the outside of each binder.
2. Store related information within one binder.
3. Use dividers within each binder to separate the various sections.
4. Keep a three-hole punch accessible to make it easy to quickly punch holes in the papers and put them in binders.

If you prefer using binders but have more file space than shelf space, there is a way around this problem. Buy plastic binders that hang on file rods.

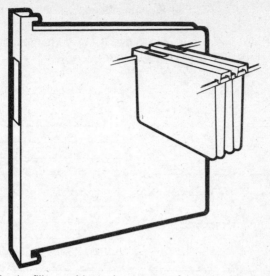

Store notebooks in filing cabinets by means of hanging binders. (Courtesy of Globe-Weis)

GETTING STARTED

The most difficult part of implementing a new filing system is getting started. Go back to your filing cabinet and start thinking about the best filing system for you. Make copies of the chart on page 142 and use it to plan your own filing system.

When you are completely overhauling your files, it's helpful to get your new system down on paper before you start labeling files. You'll have fewer surprises, and you'll spend less time moving tabs around and working in folders you forgot about.

File Planning Chart

Use this chart to write down the contents of your files before you go through the process of labeling your folders.

Main Category   Subcategories

_____   _____
                                       _____
                                       _____
_____   _____
                                       _____
_____   _____
                                       _____
                                       _____
_____   _____
                                       _____
_____   _____
                                       _____
                                       _____
_____   _____
                                       _____
_____   _____
                                       _____
                                       _____
_____   _____
                                       _____
                                       _____

QUICK TIP FOR HOME OFFICE PROFESSIONALS

The Three-Minute Paper Test. If you can't retrieve any piece of paper you need within three minutes, your filing system isn't working. Taking more than three minutes to find a document is like taking the local train through all stops when you could have taken an express. As a home office professional, you don't have that kind of time to waste.

TROUBLESHOOTING YOUR FILES

In my years of helping clients organize their offices, I've discovered a few problems associated with filing. The following are the most common, with the solutions I've devised for them.

Problem: File folders are sticking out of the top of hanging folders.

Solution: Limit yourself to six interior folders within a hanging folder. When a hanging folder gets to be one and a half to two inches thick, start a new one. Another option is to use a box-bottom hanging folder.

Problem: An interior folder that is too full.

Solution: Divide the papers into separate interior files, then put them in one hanging folder labeled with a name that describes the overall category of the interior files.

Problem: Can't see the tabs on hanging folders.

Solution: Use file folders that are cut lower. Also, make sure your papers are completely in the folder before you put it away.

Problem: Too many places to look for a particular piece of paper.

Solution: You are probably using too many hanging folders and too many interior folders. Look at your interior files and see which ones could be grouped together in one hanging folder. Don't start a separate interior folder until you have accumulated eight pages of related information. Until that point, group papers with others.

Problem: After taking a file out, you don't know where it belongs.

Solution: This is less likely to occur if you keep hanging folders in the filing cabinet and take out only the interior file. If you're still having trouble, make sure you keep a thorough index of your files. It may also help to color coordinate your interior folders so that all folders in one file drawer are the same color.

Problem: Losing papers between hanging folders.

Solution: Make sure you use interior folders within hanging folders and always place your papers in an interior file. Some hanging folders are a lighter color inside to help you see that you are placing a file inside, rather than outside, the hanging folder. There are also connectors available that join one hanging folder to another, making it impossible to lose papers between hanging folders.

Problem: You need to have personal files accessible, but you can't free up an entire file drawer for them.

Solution: Get another filing cabinet (or vertical file holder, or file cart). Don't put personal papers in the same file drawer as your work-related papers.

Problem: The file drawer is too full and you can't move the folders back and forth in order to take interior folders out.

Solution: Leave about an inch leeway in the file drawer so the folders have room to move.

Problem: You have to shuffle through the folder to find the most current papers.

Solution: Keep the most recent papers in front where they are readily available.

TOWARD A PAPERLESS BUSINESS ENVIRONMENT

For years there has been talk of a "paperless society," an ideal world in which all you would need to do is press a button on a computer to retrieve any information you needed. It looks as if we won't be paperless for a while, not because of the technology needed (it exists), but because of our habits.

Electronic mail (E-mail) replaces the standard memo as a way of conveying information. Sales reps often stay in contact with their corporate office by means of E-mail. I have worked with reps, however, who insisted on printing out hard-copy versions of computer transmissions, which defeats the purpose of the E-mail system.

If you need to see pieces of paper in front of you, rather than read your information on a computer screen, it's important that you learn how to efficiently handle the paper that continually flows into your home office. This is why the next chapter is devoted to handling incoming information.

10 ◰ ◰ ◰

HANDLING INCOMING INFORMATION EFFICIENTLY

Some papers, such as mail, magazines, business cards, newspapers, and books, fall somewhere between "current" and "reference." Many people find that this is the most difficult type of information to categorize. That's why it usually ends up in stacks on, next to, or around your desk.

A real estate agent at one of my seminars admitted that he used to be so overwhelmed by the volume of his incoming mail that he just let it accumulate everywhere. Magazines, letters, and newspapers were scattered all over his office. One day he returned home to find police searching through his office. His mother-in-law, who had come to visit, had taken a look at his office and was certain he'd been robbed.

Before bringing anything into your home office, throw out any mail you know you'll never look at again. This alone will cut down on clutter tremendously.

The best way to deal with mail is to spend a few minutes each day processing it. This means taking the time to open each envelope, make a decision on it (remember P-A-P-E-R: put it in a stacking bin, act on it, put it in a file, enter it on your "to do" list and file it, or rid yourself of it), and move on to the next piece.

USING A POSTAL SERVICE

A good way to reduce the amount of information that comes into your home is to pick up your business mail elsewhere. Using a postal service such as Mail Boxes, Etc. is similar to having a post office box, but instead of having a post office box number, you can get a suite number. There are a number of advantages to this approach.

- You can sort through your mail while you're there and take home only the information you need.
- Your business mail will be delivered separately from your personal mail.
- No one will know your home address, which will keep clients and salespeople from showing up at your door.
- A suite number gives a more professional impression than a post office box number. Some people are wary of a business that has a post office box number in its address.
- The postal service will accept packages for you and sign for them.
- A postal service allows you to mail packages by overnight express, send and receive fax transmissions, copy papers, and send packages by various means.

Disadvantages are that you have to drive somewhere to get your mail, and that there's a small overcharge when you buy stamps from a postal service instead of directly from the post office.

MAIL HANDLING TIPS

We receive far too much mail. According to the United States Postal Service, Americans receive 63 billion pieces of third-class mail—and throw out an estimated 15 percent of it unopened. The other 85 percent generates a lot of clutter. To deal with the constant flow of mail coming into your office, I recommend that you do the following:

1. Take the mail straight to your office instead of opening it elsewhere in your home. When you open mail at your desk, you'll reduce the risk of los-

ing important papers, it will be easier for you to make decisions, and you'll easily be able to put the sorted mail where it belongs.

2. Designate one place, preferably your "to sort" bin, for all of your incoming mail. You could use a wicker basket kept near or under your desk, or stacking trays kept on a filing cabinet. Choose a spot other than your desktop. Don't use an "in" basket on your desk, because it will fill up quickly with unsorted material—and that leads to unnecessary distractions.

3. Always open your mail at the same place, at your desk and next to a wastebasket. Opening your mail next to the wastebasket makes it easier to throw out right away what you don't need.

4. Open all of your mail at one sitting. This takes a few minutes, but saves time in the long run. Open each piece of mail, make a decision about it, and move on to the next piece. If you stop to make a phone call or to do something else, this process will take longer than it needs to. When your mind is set on a task, that task will be completed sooner if you stay focused on it.

5. Read each piece of mail long enough to know what action is required and by what date. If you don't bother to read invitations, notices, and announcements, you may miss out on various meetings and time-sensitive opportunities.

6. Make as many decisions right away as you can. If you put something aside "until later," you've already made the decision not to decide.

7. Throw out any unnecessary papers, envelopes, and enclosures and save only the vital documents you need.

8. A fast way to respond to certain types of correspondence is to write a note at the bottom of the letter and send it back. Many people would rather receive a prompt response written at the bottom of a letter than a delayed, formal response. If you want to keep a record of this correspondence, all you have to do is photocopy this sheet of paper.

9. Remember to record on your "to do" list any action you need to take before you file any papers away. If you put papers in your current files without making a note of them, you're no better off than you were when your papers were in stacks all over your desk.

The only way to be in control of your mail is to handle it on a regular basis and to get into the habit of making immediate decisions on each piece. At that point, you may actually look forward to getting the mail.

Keep in mind that your name is being bought and sold on a regular basis. If you order merchandise by mail, you are a prime candidate to receive many mail order catalogues. To cut down on the volume of this type of mail you receive, send a letter to the following organization and request that your name be removed from mail order lists:

> Direct Marketing Association, Inc.
> Mail Preference Service
> 11 West 42nd Street
> P.O. Box 3861
> New York, N.Y. 10163-3861

HOW TO DEAL WITH MAGAZINES

We are a society that generates endless amounts of information. There is a magazine for almost any interest, from scuba diving to stamp collecting. Some are hard to resist, and you may end up subscribing to too many. When that happens, you run out of time to read them all.

When your magazines start to accumulate, your level of guilt over not reading them increases proportionally. It's important for you to realize that it is simply not possible for you to read everything you would like to read. When you take that pressure off yourself, you can become more selective about what you read. To lessen your guilt, and your stacks of magazines, I recommend that you do the following:

1. Limit the number of subscription magazines you receive. When a subscription comes up for renewal, take this opportunity to determine whether or not you regularly read it. Keep in mind that if you ever need to refer to an article, you can look it up in the library on microfilm and quickly make a copy.
2. Keep your personal magazines stored in one place with other personal magazines and catalogues, preferably somewhere other than your home office.
3. Keep your professional magazines in your "to read" stacking bin or another designated spot until you are ready to read them. Absolutely keep them off your desk and out of the way of your papers in progress.
4. Go through your reading bin once a week and tear out the articles you will read at a later date. Put these articles in a folder labeled "to read" and keep the folder in the bin or in your briefcase if you use it daily. When you

leave for an appointment, grab the folder and go. After you've read an article, either throw it away, put it in your "to file" bin, or file it.

5. If you don't want to rip up your magazines, make copies of the articles you want to read. Then file the magazines in a magazine holder labeled with the name of the magazine and the year.

6. Another alternative is to highlight on the magazine's table of contents the articles you want to read. Keep the magazine in your "to read" bin until you have a chance to get to it. As you read the article, highlight the important parts for reference later.

7. When you file magazines, put a detachable note on the outside cover listing the articles you may need to refer to later.

8. Keep only a year's worth of magazines. When the new year starts, replace the first issue you stored with the new issue. Remember, the library has plenty of room to store magazines. For catalogues, keep only one season's worth. When you get a second, throw away the first.

9. Purchase magazines on computer disks. Many publications offer the alternative of receiving disks instead of the magazine. Instead of stacks of magazines, you'll have a few computer disks.

Sturdy plastic file boxes can be used to organize magazines and catalogues. (Courtesy of Esselte Pendaflex Corporation)

QUICK TIP FOR HOME OFFICE PROFESSIONALS

Set aside time each week to read. Schedule it on your calendar. Even spending half an hour or an hour each morning reading makes a big difference in getting through all of the newspapers, professional publications, sales information, brochures, and other material you need to read.

HOW TO DEAL WITH NEWSPAPERS

Newspapers are short-lived, in that they're history after a few days. Yet so many people hold onto them until they get the opportunity to read them. If you haven't read the newspapers stacked in your home office (or kitchen, or another part of your house) after three days, toss them or recycle them. The following are a few tips to help you save time handling newspapers:

1. Determine whether you should continue receiving the newspaper. You can do this quickly by looking at your newspaper recycling pile. If all, or almost all, of the daily newspapers are unread, cancel your subscription and buy the paper only on Sunday. If newspapers only distract you from working, cancel your subscription.

2. When you receive the newspaper, bring it into your home office (if no one else will be reading it), take out the sections you plan to read, and put them in your "to read" bin. Then get rid of the rest of the paper.

3. When you go through the paper, cut out any articles you want to keep. If someone else will be reading the paper after you, place a check mark next to the articles you want to save, and when the other reader is through, cut them out. You'll save time searching for these articles by making a note on the front page of the section where an article is located.

4. After you've cut out an article, write on the right-hand corner where it will be filed. If it's an article you would like to keep for some time, make a photocopy of the original because the original will eventually yellow.

5. As you read an article, highlight the points you will refer to again. When you go back to the article, you'll be able to go right to the "meat" of it.

6. If you have a modem, consider subscribing to CompuServe's Executive News Service. It carries news items from the Associated Press news wire,

The Washington Post, and other news sources. It gives you straight news, without all of the extra features and advertising.

HOW TO HANDLE BUSINESS CARDS

Business cards are a blessing because they're an easy and inexpensive way to market your home-based business, but they become a curse when the business cards you receive in return start to accumulate. You can either refuse to accept them, keep them in a drawer with a rubber band around them, or organize them.

A card holder such as a Rolodex is an efficient way to file business cards. When cards are stored vertically in a holder, they're easy to flip through. There are a variety of products you may want to use in conjunction with your card file.

- Consider buying clear or colored plastic sleeves that fit over the business cards and attach to the bottom of the card file.
- There is a punch available that strategically places two holes in a business card to allow you to file it quickly. This way you don't have to copy the information on a blank card and store the original elsewhere. This also beats cutting and attaching a business card by hand.
- Another product—a plastic adhesive strip with holes in it— attaches to the bottom of a business card so you can file it directly in the card file.

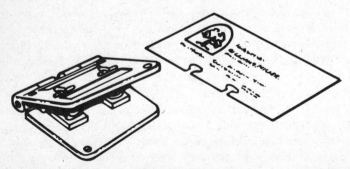

A special punch adds holes to business cards so that they can be placed directly in a business card file. (Courtesy of Merrick Industries Inc.)

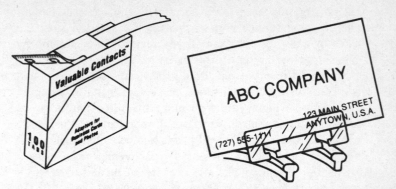

Plastic tabs attach to the bottom of business cards so that they can be placed in a business card file. (Courtesy of Merrick Industries Inc.)

■ If you have a 3″ × 5″ card file—larger than business card size—staple or tape a business card to the left-hand side of a card, leaving space on the right-hand side for personal information about the person (e.g., the secretary's name, a spouse's name, birthdays).

When you file a business card, you can file it under either the name of the business or the name of the individual. Choose whichever approach will come to your mind first when you need to retrieve the information.

When copying information onto a blank file card, put the phone number in the upper right-hand corner of the card to make it easy to see. You have to push the file open further to read a number written at the bottom of a card.

Keep business cards you receive while traveling in an envelope in your personal planner. Then file them when you get home.

Save business cards that need to be filed in the front of your card file or in a small container next to your card file. Then file them once a week. In addition to a business card file for your desk, there are other options that might work well for you.

■ A business card book, available in 8½″ × 11″ or smaller, keeps business cards stored in plastic sleeves. It's not practical to alphabetize the cards throughout the book, in that each time you get a new business card you have to move every card. Instead, keep a page for the *A*'s, one for the *B*'s, and so on. Then alphabetize the cards within each page. Or you can store the cards by category (for example, by region of the country, by supplier, or by the service offered).

■ If you travel regularly and need to have important names and addresses with you at all times, make sure that after filing an important business card you enter the information in the addresses/phone numbers section of your daily planner. (Use pencil, because addresses and phone numbers often change.) If you keep names and addresses in your planner only, make a photocopy of your address sheets every six months in case you lose your planner. When you make an updated copy, toss the old one. The new copy gets filed in your reference files.

■ Electronic name and address holders make the storage of important information easy. Their only drawback is the amount of time it takes to enter this information initially. However, you save time on the retrieval end.

■ There are computer programs that store names and addresses as one of their many features. Telemagic and ACT! are two. Before you leave town, you just print out the names you need and keep the updated list with you. If you have the list reduced to fit your planner, it is extremely convenient to use. Computerizing your business card information saves space because you don't need to keep the original business cards once the information is entered in your computer.

Debbie, a sales rep, was away from her home office from Monday through Friday, three weeks out of each month. Because she was rarely home, she had to keep all of her clients' names with her at all times. She was constantly updating her client list by hand, to the point where she could hardly read it. Each time she acquired a new client, she would transfer the information from her client's card to her list. She kept telling herself that she would rewrite her list, but she never found the time to do it. I suggested that she use a computer program to keep her list up to date.

Now when Debbie meets a new client, she enters his or her name in her laptop computer and always has those names with her on a disk. To avoid duplicating information, she throws away business cards after she has entered the information. On weekends when she is home, Debbie backs up her disks.

Go through your business card file or printout at least twice a year and remove the cards or names you no longer need.

KEEPING BOOKS UNDER CONTROL

No matter where you turn, someone is always talking about or recommending a book. To many, being in a bookstore is like being in a candy store—there are so many to choose from, and you want them all.

Before you buy a book, ask yourself why you want it. Are you buying it because it's a best-seller and you know everyone will be talking about it, or does it deal with a topic that interests you? Will it increase your income or just distract you when you should be working? The following are some tips on keeping your books under control:

■ Go through the books you own now and pull out any you know you won't read, then give them away or sell them. Bookstores throughout the country buy used books. You won't get rich on the money you make, but think of the space you'll save in your office.

■ Check books out of the library instead of buying them. In addition to saving money, you'll have an incentive to read the book before it's due back. When you check out a book, make a note in your daily planner a few days before the due date to give yourself a chance to finish it.

■ Listen to books on tape. This is a good way to save time while keeping up on the latest books. There are companies that summarize on tape the books you want to read but don't have time to read. You could listen to them while you are in your office, in your car, or exercising.

■ Invest in a sturdy bookcase. If your books are out of sight, they'll definitely be out of mind, and you'll never read or even refer to them. Arrange books on your bookcase (1) alphabetically by author, (2) alphabetically by title in general categories (e.g., business, personal, motivational), or (3) alphabetically by title according to subject (e.g., sales, marketing, computers).

■ You can distinguish categories of books by putting a different colored dot on the spine of each one. If you file your books alphabetically by author, refiling is easy if you use a different colored dot for each letter of the alphabet. If you file your books by general category or subject, use a different color for each one. When a book covers several areas, put a colored dot on the spine for each area.

■ When you read a book, highlight a point you want to remember. Use a highlighter pen that doesn't bleed through to the next page. Then add a word at the top of the page to take you to that place. Another option is to use a detachable note that sticks out of the edge of the book.

Operating a home office involves a lot of expenses, from printing to postage. Spending the money is easy. Keeping track of where you've spent it is a challenge. In the next chapter, you'll learn ways to track your expenses that will save you many frustrating hours at tax time.

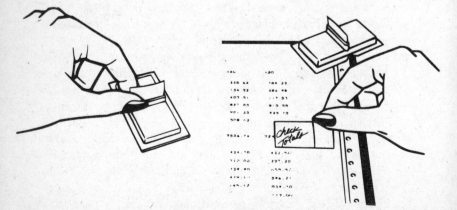

Small, detachable notes are useful for flagging information in books and notebooks. (Courtesy of 3M Commercial Office Supply Division)

QUICK TIP FOR HOME OFFICE PROFESSIONALS

Streamline wherever you can. Take a racer's approach to office organizing: every second you can trim from your day means a more rapid approach to the finish line.

- Toss out any papers you can.
- Move paper forward each time you handle it.
- Drop meaningless tasks from your "to do" list.
- Learn the fine art of ignoring problems that will solve themselves or will never be solved.
- Minimize the time you spend looking for things.
- Use it or lose it. Anything you don't use doesn't belong in your office.

11

ORGANIZING RECEIPTS

Receipts come in many sizes, from small cash register receipts to large invoices. Most people stash their receipts in a shoebox throughout the year and deal with them near tax time or before the deadline their accountant gives them. The inconvenience comes when it's time to sort through the receipts and prepare your tax return. Instead of spending time on your business, you have to take a day or a week to divide your receipts, to make sure they are properly recorded, and to total them.

Whether you own your own business or are a corporate employee in a home office, you will need to pay taxes. Keeping track of your receipts will ensure that you get all of the deductions to which you are entitled. If you are a corporate employee, you will be reimbursed for the amount of money you spend on company expenses.

Natalie, a computer programmer who attended one of my seminars, was transferred from a corporate office to her home. After two years of working at home, she added up all of the money she had spent on office supplies and discovered that her receipts totaled $450. Realizing that this represented serious money, she belatedly turned in her receipts—and was refused reimbursement because she'd had them for so long. If she had been in control of her receipts sooner, she would have been $450 richer. If you're an entrepreneur, you will want to do the following:

- Keep track of all of your expenses in order to document how company money was spent.
- Use most of your receipts at the end of the year in preparing your tax return.
- Maintain receipts so you can produce the ones you claimed as deductions if you are audited.

If you're a corporate employee, you will want to do the following:

- Keep track of your expenses so that you can be reimbursed by your employer.
- Use only a few receipts at the end of the year in preparing your tax return, depending upon how many were reimbursed.
- Be able to obtain reimbursement and expense records from the corporate office were you to be audited.

QUICK TIP FOR HOME OFFICE PROFESSIONALS

Keep one credit card for business expenses and one for personal expenses. This way there will be no question about whether an item was a business or personal expense.

KEEPING TRACK OF RECEIPTS

Doing your taxes should not be a long, drawn out process. If you take the time to organize your receipts during the year, you'll see at least three benefits.

1. You'll shorten the amount of time you spend preparing your taxes.
2. If you use an accountant, you'll significantly reduce your bill, as he will spend less time sorting through your receipts. If your accountant has to look through hundreds of receipts, your bill will be tremendous.
3. You'll be able to see throughout the year how much money you're spending.

During the day, keep an envelope with you at all times to hold receipts from business expenses you incur. On meal receipts, be sure to write the name of the person, company, title, type of meal, and reason for the meeting. Then, at least once a week, process these receipts by recording their amounts and filing them away. It's unrealistic to think that you will be able to record your receipts daily. Instead, keep them in a folder labeled Receipts to Enter.

After you've recorded your expenses, there are a few ways you can store receipts to prevent them from becoming a major nuisance and to minimize the time it takes to organize them for tax purposes. Whatever method you choose, the key is to keep your receipts under control by keeping them in a specific place so that you'll be able to organize them at tax time with the least amount of time and effort. It's important to choose a receipt filing system with which you are comfortable, and to keep it as simple as possible. The more difficult it is to use, the less likely you will be to use it.

If handling finances is not your strength, hire a bookkeeper to track your finances and manage your receipts. The amount of money you spend on a bookkeeper will be considerably less than the amount of time you would waste trying to handle your own records.

USING FILES

When you store your receipts in files, they are readily accessible. Even more important, you can file them by main categories and subcategories. This is helpful when you're preparing a tax return because all of your receipts will already be broken down by subcategory. It's also helpful when you need to track down a specific receipt, in that you won't have to look through all of your receipts to find it.

I recommend using hanging folders to file your receipts because they accommodate interior folders for the subcategories you select. If you don't have room for hanging folders, you'll have to use expandable (accordion) folders.

The easiest method for filing receipts is by category. The following are tips for using a categorical filing system for your receipts:

1. Label a hanging folder Expense Records. Inside, place an interior folder labeled Expenses. Place inside the interior folder one expense sheet for each category of expenses.

2. Label hanging folders for your main categories (for example, Car).

3. Label interior folders for your subcategories (for example, Insurance, Maintenance, and Mileage) and place them in the hanging folders.

4. Each time you get a receipt, place it in the appropriate folder after recording it on the expense sheet for that category.

5. At the end of the year, take the receipts out of each interior folder, staple them together by category, and store them in a manila envelope. Label the envelope Taxes and include the year. You'll use the expense sheets to complete your tax return.

Another option is to store receipts in a number 10 envelope by category and to put all of the envelopes in a large manila envelope labeled Taxes (and year). Still another option is to file your receipts by month, although this is almost never an efficient way to keep receipts. It makes it difficult to locate an individual receipt (you have to hunt through all of the files until you find it), and at the end of the year you will need to go through all of your monthly files and divide your expenses by category to get monthly totals. This means you end up handling your receipts several times.

The only time that filing receipts by month will work for you is if you have only a few receipts to store each month (up to four). Otherwise you'll end up sorting and organizing at tax time, which is a process you want to avoid.

USING BINDERS

The binder receipt system works much the same way as the file system, but the receipts are stored in a binder instead of a file. Set up this system as follows:

1. Start with a three-ring binder.

2. Put as many subject dividers inside the binder as you think you'll need. Label each divider with a main category (for example, Office Supplies, Postage, Car).

3. Insert an expense sheet behind each divider. You can buy these preprinted or make them up yourself. At the top of each expense sheet, write the name of the appropriate category.

EXPENSES

Category _____

Date	Description	Charges	Balance

Use a sheet like this one for recording your expenses in each category.

4. You'll need an envelope for each category in which to store receipts. A business-size envelope is adequate, although a manila 6″ × 9″ envelope is even better. Punch holes in the side of the envelope, write the name of the category on the front, and place it in the binder behind the corresponding divider and receipt ledger.

5. Each week, take the expense receipts out of your daily planner or Receipts to Enter folder and sort them into your binder. Remember to record each one before putting it in the envelope.

The advantage of this approach is that when you are ready to prepare your taxes, you'll have a complete ledger detailing all of your expenses by category, and your receipts will be in corresponding envelopes. All you will need to do is give your accountant the ledgers and store the receipts in a box labeled with Tax Information and the year.

USING ENVELOPES

This system uses envelopes instead of file folders. This is a good option for you if you have only limited file space. This system is easy to use, and at the end of the year your receipts are all neatly tucked into envelopes, ready to be stored with your tax information.

Set up this system as follows:

1. Start with enough envelopes for all of your expense categories. (There are no main categories and subcategories with this system.) Business-size envelopes are adequate, but 6″ × 9″ manila envelopes are better.

2. Label each envelope with the name of an expense category.

3. When you get a receipt, record the expense on the outside of the envelope and put the receipt inside. An alternative is to use a separate ledger to record your expenses before filing your receipts in the envelopes.

4. Store the envelopes either in a hanging folder or in a box labeled Receipts.

COMPUTERIZED RECORDKEEPING

The amount of paperwork involved in accounting keeps many people from bothering with it until the last minute. There are various computer programs available that can help you keep track of your expenses and finances.

William, a home-based photographer, used to spend hours balancing his checkbook and tracking his expenses. I recommended that he use a software program called "Quicken," which, among other tasks, helps you balance your checkbook and reconcile your checkbook with your bank statement. What used to take William hours each month now takes only twenty minutes, and at tax time the program totals his expenses by category effortlessly. There are definitely benefits to using a computerized system.

- There is less room for error because you aren't doing all of the arithmetic.
- There is no paper involved until you print out your end-of-the-year statement.
- At any time you can tell how much you are spending and where.

If computerized recordkeeping interests you, take the time to investigate the various software programs now available to make sure that the one you buy fits your needs and is one you will use. Once you start using it, be careful not to set up too many categories; making your system unnecessarily complicated defeats your intention, which is to simplify your life. Also, keep in mind that you'll still need a method for storing your receipts. Any of the methods previously mentioned will work for you.

SAMPLE CATEGORIES FOR FILING RECEIPTS

Use the following categories as a guide when setting up your receipt filing system. Use hanging folders for main categories and interior folders for subcategories. If you chose a filing system that doesn't make use of main categories, use just the subcategories.

Hanging Folder	**Interior Folder**
Administrative Expenses	Office Supplies Postage Printing
Automobile Expenses	Maintenance Mileage
Client Expenses	Gifts Meals and Entertainment
Contributions	Charitable Contributions Donated Merchandise
Education	Association Dues Seminars Classes
Home Office	Rent or House Payment Repairs
Insurance	Car Home Life Medical
Interest on Loans	Bank Loans Charge Accounts Office Equipment Small Business Association
Investments	Pension and Profit-Sharing SEP Contributions

Hanging Folder	Interior Folder	
Invoices	A–D E–H I–L　　or M–P Q–Z	Client A Client B Client C
Marketing	Advertising Marketing	
Miscellaneous	Laundry and Cleaning Legal and Professional Fees	
Operating Expenses	Equipment Purchases/Leasing Long-Distance Calls Safe Deposit Box Rental	
Travel Expenses	Airfare Car Rental Lodging	
Utilities	Electric Gas Water	

WHICH DOCUMENTS YOU NEED TO KEEP AND FOR HOW LONG

During my seminars I am often asked about what receipts or documentation a home office professional needs to keep and for how long. The general statute of limitations for the Internal Revenue Service is three years; however, this varies from state to state. The IRS can go back as far as seven years and, if they suspect fraud, they may go back as far as they like. I recommend that you keep your cancelled checks and tax return information for seven years (and that you avoid defrauding the government). If you are still unsure about what to keep, contact your local IRS office and your certified public accountant.

After you have completed your income tax form, make a copy of it. Mail the original to the government, and keep your copy, with all of your documentation and receipts, in a manila envelope or, if it doesn't fit, in an accordion file. Store past returns in a storage box, separated by year, and label the outside of the box.

TIPS FOR DEALING WITH THE INTERNAL REVENUE SERVICE

You can help avoid problems with the Internal Revenue Service (IRS) by keeping thorough records of your business expenses and by understanding business deductions and their limitations. For example, if you are claiming a portion of your home for business use, make sure that the room is being used only for business purposes. A foldout bed in your office will prevent you from being able to legitimately claim a spare room for business use exclusively.

If you are audited, you want to be helpful and accommodating to the IRS auditor, but you also don't want to pay any more taxes than you have to. With this in mind, the following are tips for handling the auditing process:

1. If you are audited, bring representation with you (your certified public accountant [CPA] or bookkeeper). They know how to deal with the IRS and will have a good idea of the questions the IRS will ask you.
2. If you go alone to the audit, do not automatically answer every question you are asked. If, for example, the auditor asks you how much you spent on gasoline last year and you don't know, it's okay to tell the auditor that you will find out and let him or her know. If you make a guess and it's incorrect, that information may be used against you.
3. Don't panic. If you've kept good records while you've been in business, you shouldn't have anything to worry about. If you haven't keep good records, it's never too late to start. An audit could provide just the motivation you've needed.

USING A CERTIFIED PUBLIC ACCOUNTANT

Hiring a CPA is one of the best investments you can make. You'll save yourself time in preparing taxes and, more important, you'll protect yourself to a certain degree from being audited by the IRS. The following tips will make it easier for you to work with your CPA:

1. Make your tax information easy for your CPA to understand.
2. Rather than hand your CPA a shoebox full of receipts, separate the receipts, record the totals for each category, and give your accountant the totals. If you've set up a system for handling receipts as described earlier, all you have to do is total the expenses. Your CPA does not need to see your individual receipts, but you do need to hold onto them in the event that you are audited.
3. If your records are incomplete and you're missing receipts, use your check register to pull out checks that are tax deductible. Then give your CPA a copy of your check register, with the tax deductible checks highlighted and the type of expense indicated. He or she doesn't need to see the actual cancelled checks.
4. If you're missing receipts for items you charged, give your CPA a copy of your charge card statements, with the tax deductible charges highlighted and the type of expense explained. Some credit card companies prepare a year-end summary for you.

HOW TO SAVE BANK STATEMENTS AND CANCELLED CHECKS

You'll save time at tax time if you handle your bank statements and cancelled checks just once, at the end of the month. It's a good idea to keep a separate checking account for business expenses; this way there is no confusion about which expenses are personal and which are work-related, either in your mind or in the mind of the IRS.

You don't need to store banking deposit slips. Keep them only until you have checked them off the next monthly bank statement. You do, however, need to set up a system for storing bank statements and cancelled checks. For these you have two options: binders or folders.

■ The Binder Method

1. In your checkbook register, mark off the checks that have cleared, then balance your checkbook.
2. Store the bank statements in a three-ring binder labeled with the year.

3. Keep the cancelled checks in a small accordion file labeled either by month or by category of expense.

How you file your cancelled checks depends on how your mind works. If you need to find a cancelled check and the only thing you remember is the type of expense (not the date), storing your cancelled checks categorically will make it easier for you to find the checks you need.

■ The File Method

1. Label a hanging folder Bank/Checks.
2. Label an interior folder Bank Statements and file your statements there.
3. Label more interior folders either with the names of your expense categories or with the names of the month. File your cancelled checks in them. Depending on the number of checks you write each month, you may want to use a box-bottom folder.

TIPS FOR MAKING TAX TIME EASIER

Beth Denton, CPA and president of Denton Wolter & Company, a Dallas accounting firm, makes the following suggestions to make tax time easier:

1. Document the miles you drive for business purposes.
2. Use your daily planner as backup documentation. If you have recorded your mileage throughout the year and are questioned about how many miles you drove, your planner will show your various appointments.
3. Remember to send 1099 forms to any unincorporated entity to which you have made payments of $600 or more (i.e., consultants or contractors). If you don't, you'll have to pay a penalty.
4. Don't wait until a few days before April 15 to turn in your tax information to your accountant. This does not give your accountant enough time to complete your return before the tax deadline.
5. Keep a list of your stocks, CDs, and money market accounts so that you'll know what statements you need at the end of the year. If you forget to report information about these accounts, you'll have to pay penalties.

KEEPING TRACK OF PETTY CASH

There are times when you need to buy something—from a postage stamp to a $2 magazine—for which you don't write a check. You need to keep track of these expenses, either for tax purposes (if you're self-employed) or for reimbursement purposes (if you're a home-based corporate employee). There are two ways to use petty cash.

1. Cash a check for $30 (make it out to cash). In your check register, make sure it is clearly labeled Petty Cash to eliminate questions at tax time. Keep the money in a small box or in an envelope inside a file folder labeled Petty Cash. Before you make a small purchase, take out the money you need. After you've made your purchase, put the receipt and any change back in the petty cash box or file. Write on the receipt what was purchased.
2. Your other option is to set up a petty cash box as in number 1, but to use your personal money to buy what you need and then reimburse yourself from your petty cash box later. If you work for a corporation, turn in all of your petty cash receipts at once, either each month or every few months, depending upon the amount, to get reimbursed.

When the petty cash is down to $5, balance the receipts and write another check for $30 and follow the same procedure as before. Do not consider petty cash as money to use on a regular basis. It is only to be used as a way to avoid writing checks for only a few dollars and as a means of fast reimbursement.

Keeping track of your receipts on a regular basis is one of those tasks that people often put aside because they "don't have time." The tips in the following chapter should help you gain better control over how you use your time so that routine matters don't turn into organizational nightmares.

12

☑ ☑ ☑

MAKING
BETTER USE
OF YOUR TIME

Winston Churchill said, "Time is one thing that can never be retrieved. One may lose and regain a friend, one may lose and regain money; opportunity once spurned may come again, but the hours that are lost in idleness can never be brought back to be used in gainful pursuits."

To see how much time you are wasting that could be spent on gainful pursuits, you need to track your activities for an entire day, hour by hour. Using the chart on page 172, do this for one day this week, and then do it for another day next week. After you've taken the time to record and analyze how you're spending your time, you can then work to eliminate those activities that are time wasters or to reschedule tasks so that your time is used more efficiently.

If you find it difficult to get excited about the idea of tracking your activities for a day, think about how nice it would be to have enough time to finish that project you're working on, or to start that project you've been talking about, or even to take some time off for once. The key to accomplishing more is to make better use of the hours you have available each day.

Evaluating Your Use of Time

Activities

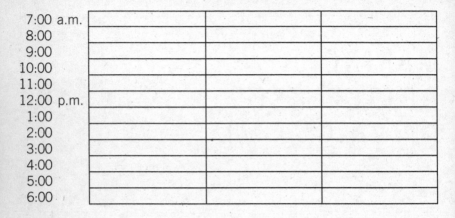

7:00 a.m.			
8:00			
9:00			
10:00			
11:00			
12:00 p.m.			
1:00			
2:00			
3:00			
4:00			
5:00			
6:00			

HOW TO MAKE BETTER USE OF YOUR TIME

Time management is an overused and misunderstood term. It's not possible to control time; there are only 24 hours in each day and 168 hours in each week. It is possible, however, to control what you do with your time. Making better use of your time will help you overcome the feeling that you're running in place: you have a list a mile long, and no matter how hard you work, you never seem to accomplish as much as you should.

Throughout the day, ask yourself if what you are doing is the best use of your time. Every few hours, stop what you're doing and decide if the task you're working on is the one that needs to be done today or if it is one that could be done at a later date. You don't have to check up on yourself more often than every three hours; frequent checks would be disruptive. Set the alarm on your watch, or set a timer to go off, or set the alarm on your computer if you're going to be home most of the day.

Determine your best time of day and schedule important tasks for that time. Some people jump out of bed at 5:00 each morning and are ready to go, whereas others aren't able to function well until the afternoon. Concentrate on important tasks during the time you're most productive. Leave the less important tasks for when your energy level is low.

Jerry Bittle, creator of the internationally syndicated comic strip "Geech," adjusts his schedule to fulfill his creative need and to fit in with his family's schedule. He works from 8:00 each weeknight until 3:30 each morning, then sleeps until about 11:00. When his children get home from school, he's available to spend time with them. He prefers working at night because he is a night owl, the type of person who perks up in the evening. Moreover, while he works, everyone else is asleep and he's not interrupted. His schedule is unlike that of anyone else I've ever known, yet it makes perfect sense for him.

Stay focused on the activity at hand. Many of us tend to start one project and then bounce to another without finishing the first. At the end of the day, it's possible to feel exhausted without having accomplished anything. The problem is a lack of focus. When you focus on the project you're working on, you can complete it faster.

Kristine, a sales rep for a gift company, was excited about finally organizing her home office. As we worked together on organizing her desk drawers, she would start on one, then jump to another, then skip to a third. I persuaded Kristine to get back to the first drawer, and after that we started getting somewhere. When we were finished, we had a little talk about using time wisely. Kristine's misguided enthusiasm had helped me see how she had gotten so disorganized in the first place.

Schedule at least one full day a week in the office. If you spend a majority of your time out of the office, set aside one day to spend in your office catching up on paperwork, making phone calls, and planning the following week. Determine which day of the week is slower for you in terms of phone calls you receive or appointments you make, and make that the day you spend in your office. You may have to make an effort to keep that day clear, but if you do, the rest of your week will go more smoothly.

Make appointments with yourself to work on certain tasks. Treat yourself as you would a client, and put yourself on your calendar. Block out certain time periods when you will work on specific tasks. The task could be a monthly report, a client proposal, or a marketing plan—something that needs to be done and that needs your full attention. Treat this time as an appointment to keep, and make it a productive session. During this time, turn on your answering machine and concentrate only on the project you've scheduled. If you wait for an "opportune moment" to work on projects, it will never come.

Learn to say no. Do you have trouble saying no? When you don't set limits, the quality of your work suffers and your ability to maintain quality service is reduced. You end up disappointing the clients you didn't want to turn away. There's nothing wrong with being busy, until the quality of your service suffers.

Denise, a bank consultant, had so much to do that she started missing deadlines. Her home-based business had grown more quickly than she'd anticipated, but she didn't want to turn down any new clients. Soon, she was losing clients! I persuaded her to stop taking on more projects than she had time to complete and to concentrate on accomplishing her top-priority tasks first. Although it hurts to turn down work, clients are much more understanding about your being busy than they are about your missing deadlines.

Keep like with like. Group similar items so that you'll be able to find what you need immediately. File related paperwork in the same place so that you'll have fewer places to look for it. When things are scattered around your office, you end up spending more time looking for them.

It's also a good idea to group similar tasks. Run all of your calls at once so that you don't keep interrupting your work time with phone calls all day. Write all of your letters during another block of time. You'll find that they get done more quickly if you do several at once because you are able to fully concentrate on that particular type of task. When you're scheduling appointments, group them with other appointments. Schedule appointments in the same area at the same time, and avoid making two trips where one might do. Do all of your errands in one afternoon, instead of taking a little bit of time out of every afternoon. The more you group like tasks and like items together, the more efficiently you'll be using your time.

Have a place for everything. By now you know that your office should have "a place for everything, and everything in its place." Don't put things anywhere "for now," or they may end up there forever. Designate a specific place for the papers and supplies you need on a regular basis and remember to store the same types of items together. You will spend less time searching for lost items and more time accomplishing important tasks.

Take the extra few seconds to put something away where it belongs, instead of putting it near the place it belongs. Rather than putting it at the top of the basement stairs or by the door leading to the garage, take the extra minute to put it away properly. The greater number of times you handle an item before you put it away, the more time you waste.

Keep frequently used items in reach and in stock. Remember the work circle (see page 67), and keep the items you use on a regular basis within arm's reach. Even though your office may be small, each time you have to leave your desk to get something, you waste valuable time. You also leave yourself open to distractions. While you're on your way to the place you store extra supplies, you may find something else to do.

Keep track of supplies that are running low, as was discussed in Chapter 4. If you don't have enough stamps to mail your letters, or paper to print your proposal, or disks to back up your work, you'll end up wasting time while you try to set things straight.

Hire outside help if necessary. Personal service businesses continue to grow as demands on our time increase. Small business owners often don't want to hire additional people full time, so they opt for freelancers. It's easier to hire someone on a project-by-project basis than to bring someone on full time.

There comes a point when you'll realize that you can't do everything yourself. Whether the task is putting information into your computer, running errands, cleaning your house, or answering the phone, it's often better to hire someone to do it for you. A good way to decide if it's worth it is to multiply your hourly rate by the number of hours you estimate the task will take. That will make it easy to decide if it's worth your time to pay someone to do something for you. If your time could be better spent on projects and tasks that would generate income for your business, bring someone in to do the routine tasks that have to be done.

Arnold, a marketing consultant, needed to enter over 1,500 names in his computer. He kept putting off the chore because of the amount of time it would take to do it. Finally he hired a high school student to enter the names. Instead of spending his time typing, he was out of his office consulting at an hourly rate that easily covered the cost of hiring the high school student.

Some people feel it takes more time to explain how to do something than to do it themselves. Although it does take time to train someone to help you, the initial investment you make in training someone will save time in the long run. Hiring the right person will help speed this process, and so will making sure you train this person effectively.

Matthew, a freelance editor, wanted the tasks he delegated done as quickly as possible, so he would rush through his instructions. Then he would get upset when the result wasn't what he wanted. He even had trouble delegating to his children. He asked his young daughter to put the clothes in the dryer, which she did. But he didn't say anything about turning the dryer on, so she didn't. We worked on Matthew's delegating skills, and now he does the following:

- He clearly describes what he wants done.
- He asks the person to repeat his instructions back to him.
- He sets clear deadlines for completion.
- He follows up on the progress of delegated tasks.

Now Matthew finds that the projects he delegates are completed correctly and on time, leaving him with more time to work on important projects.

Allocate a few minutes at the end of each day to put away papers, clear your desk, and plan for the next day. It only takes a few minutes of "maintenance" each day to save you valuable time in the long run. Think in terms of laundry. If you let it pile up for weeks, you'll create a problem, and you'll have to spend hours washing clothes. If you wash your clothes every few days, laundry will never be a problem.

At the end of the day, take a few minutes to "close out" the day. Thursday evening, get ready for Friday. That way you won't have to face Thursday's mess when you walk in the door Friday morning. If you had a hectic day, you surely don't want to relive it the next day.

A sales rep in one of my audiences told us that the minute he opened the door to his home office, his blood pressure soared. He dreaded going into his office every morning because he knew he would waste time weeding through the previous day's mess to get to that day's work. His office caused him so much distress he would often have a headache by noon. Save yourself that anxiety by taking a few minutes to clean up.

Take time to plan. The old saying goes, "It takes money to make money." The same applies to planning. It takes time to plan, but in the long run it saves time. When you don't plan, you use time inefficiently and leave yourself open to mistakes.

Some people like the rush of adrenaline they get when they leave projects until the last minute. What they don't realize is that eventually they increase their stress level while decreasing their professionalism.

Pam, a communications specialist, felt that she worked best under pressure, so she customarily would stay up all night to finish her projects in a burst of energy. She wrote detailed proposals filled with all of the information a company would need to know about her and her company. Even though she was well qualified, she was losing every consulting bid she submitted. I looked at her proposals, and the first thing I saw was a typographical error. In rushing to complete her proposals, she was compromising the quality of her presentations. Pam started using the spell check on her computer and allowing time to proofread her proposals, and she was hired for two consulting jobs soon after that.

Failure to plan ahead can also cost you money. For example, rushing things into overnight express costs a lot more than sending them by first-class mail. When you scramble to get things done, your stress level increases and complications tend to snowball. With a plan to follow, you're less likely to run into last-minute crises.

Practice what I call "selective neglect." That's when you look at your "to do" list, realize that you can't do everything, and choose to neglect those tasks that are not important. Go to the point of completely taking them off your list.

Make it easy to start where you left off. Before you stop working on a project for the day, go one more step and bring it to a point that will make it easy for you to pick it up and finish it at a later date. Projects take longer to finish when you have to play catch-up every time you start working on them.

Follow what I call "structured flexibility." Structured flexibility is when you make your "to do" list and set your priorities, yet realize your priorities may change at any moment. Even the best plans change. Be willing to change your priorities throughout the day. It's usually easier to get the low-priority items done than it is to accomplish the important ones, so you need to make a conscious effort to concentrate on the high-priority tasks.

QUICK TIP FOR HOME OFFICE PROFESSIONALS

Confirm appointments the day before. Sometime before the next day's appointments, call to confirm each one. Sometimes people forget about appointments or wait until the day of the appointment to reschedule. Missed appointments are big time wasters, particularly if you travel to someone's office only to discover that he or she isn't there.

HABITS THAT WILL MAKE YOU MORE PRODUCTIVE

Keep the advantages of working at home from becoming disadvantages by developing habits that will make you more productive.

- *Make your environment conducive to working.* Choose an office space you enjoy, and have your office set up so that when you walk in, you can get to work.
- *Set regular office hours.* Trade show specialist Steve Miller follows the same routine every day. From 6 a.m. to 9 a.m. he makes phone calls to prospects and clients. His goal each day is to make contact with ten people. This means speaking with ten people, not just leaving messages. At 9 a.m. he shifts into what he calls his marketing mode. Everything he does from 9 a.m. until 4 p.m. relates to increasing his visibility, either through writing articles, putting together newsletters, or brainstorming. Your schedule could be very different, but the important thing is to have a certain amount of predictability about what you will accomplish, and when, during the day.
- *"Go to work" every day.* When you go into your office, treat it as you would an office away from your home. It definitely takes self-discipline to work out of your home, but the benefits make the process worthwhile.

THREE TYPES OF TIME

I divide time into the following three types:

1. *Manageable time* is when you don't have any appointments scheduled. You have the day open to use as you please. You can be flexible and productive during this time.

2. *Partially manageable time* is when you are faced with situations that take you away from your work. These situations include interruptions, doctors' appointments, and changes in your schedule that are caused by others, such as someone dropping by your house unexpectedly or a long-distance phone call from someone you haven't talked to in years. Unless you take drastic measures, there isn't much you can do to control what you accomplish during partially manageable time.

3. *Unmanageable time* is when you have specific commitments or appointments; you have to do something or be somewhere at a specific time. This is time that is already scheduled. You have no flexibility about how you use unmanageable time.

During all of these types of time, you will face interruptions, or time stealers. Knowing how to handle time stealers will determine how much you accomplish each day. Time stealers include the following:

- Incoming phone calls
- Uninvited visitors or salespeople
- Looking for lost items
- Distractions

- Equipment breakdowns
- Mail delivery
- Children
- Pets

To find out what time stealers you are particularly vulnerable to, fill out the chart on page 180. Track the time-stealers you experience for a week. Once you've recognized the types of interruptions you face, you can start to work on possible ways of dealing with them.

Time Stealers Chart

Type	Caused by Me	Caused by Others	Solution

Although some time stealers are caused by other people, many are self-generated. If your workspace is cluttered, you are more likely to become distracted (which leads to taking attention away from your work) or to lose track of items you need (which leads to spending time searching). If you have poor work habits—meaning you procrastinate and don't plan well—you'll end up rushing to meet deadlines (which leads to mistakes and more time lost). If you are unable to say no to people who are imposing on your work time, you might well find yourself going from interruption to interruption all day.

HANDLING INTERRUPTIONS

There's little you can do about important meetings, urgent deadlines, or phone calls from clients. These are a part of your work life you have to accommodate each day. Learning to handle the other types of time stealers, however, will make you a much more productive home office professional.

■ Phone Calls

There must be a law that states that when you are busiest, the phone will ring. Do you ever notice that whenever you need to get work done, the phone rings continuously? On a day when you're not so busy, you may pick up the phone a few times to make sure it still works. To control phone interruptions, I suggest that you do the following:

- *Turn on your answering machine.* Many people find it difficult to ignore a ringing phone. When you have a deadline to meet, though, you can't afford to answer every call. Keep your machine on all day, and turn up the volume so that you can screen calls as you work. You can always pick up if the call is important.

- *Try to avoid playing telephone tag.* When you leave a message on someone else's answering machine, give a specific time when you will be available to take their return call. When you record your greeting on your own answering machine, ask that the caller indicate the best time for you to return his or her call.

- *Learn how to get off the phone.* When you've finished talking and have the information you need, wind it down. If someone insists on talking, ask when you can call back.

- *Consider hiring an answering service.* If you hire an answering service to take your calls, you can forward your incoming calls to the service, which frees up your line for outgoing calls. After you get your messages, you can return calls at your convenience. Also, a service makes it look as if you have an assistant. The way a service answers the phone usually sounds as if your personal secretary is taking the call. (See Chapter 13 for more information on phone options.) The disadvantages of a service are that callers may get frustrated because your service can't answer their questions, or they may want to leave a long message or a message in their own words.

- *Take personal calls after hours.* Many people have trouble understanding the idea that home office professionals really are working during the day. You may have to inform your friends that you will not be able to take their calls during the day unless there is an emergency. Make arrangements to call them back after hours at a designated time.

■ People at Your Door

Until you work at home, it's difficult to imagine what goes on while you're away. Eventually, you'll start noticing who is home all day. If you have neighbors who like to come over to chat, make it clear that you need to work during the day. Friends and family may need gentle reminders that even though you're working at home, you are still running a business.

Ellen, an architect, was tired of commuting and decided to make the move to a home office. Her initial excitement about working at home turned to frustration when her family, who lived nearby, started dropping by for visits. They also started to take advantage of her flexible schedule, calling her to run errands for them. I suggested that Ellen discuss the situation with her family and set ground rules. Now they know that her office hours are from 8:30 a.m. to 5 p.m., and that she is not available unless there is an emergency.

■ Children

An advantage of working at home is that you get to be near your children. However, you need to place limitations on how much time you can spend with them. When you first start to work at home, your children may not understand that even though you're home, you won't be able to spend every minute with them. Although it's challenging, it is possible to have children and operate a business from home.

- ■ Expectant parents who plan to work at home after their baby arrives often figure that babies sleep all the time and therefore they will have a lot of time to work. There's no guarantee that you will get a sleepy baby, but even if you do, know that there will be many demands on your time while your child is sleeping. Moreover, if your child must sleep (or occupy himself or herself) every time you have to work, you add tremendous stress to your relationship.
- ■ Recognize from the start that if you are serious about your business, you will need some type of child care. You can't count on television or naptime to keep your child happily occupied while you work or place business phone calls. There are many child care options to investigate, from family day care (your child goes to someone else's house) to at-home

child care (a babysitter comes to your home) to a babysitting co-op (you and other parents get together and take turns watching the kids).

- If your child is of preschool age, take him or her to school in the mornings so that you have quiet time to catch up on work. Don't feel guilty that your child isn't home with you at all times. He or she needs to interact with other children.

- For those moments when your child must be with you as you take a business call, keep a box of toys nearby to distract him or her. Reserve them for emergencies so that they'll stay interesting.

- Set up a little table and chair in your office for your child to work at. Give him or her a smaller version of a telephone, stapler, tape dispenser, ruler, and safety scissors. Add plenty of paper and markers. Your child will be happy to be in the same room with you, and you'll reduce the number of items being taken out of your desk because your child will have supplies of his or her own. To protect your carpet, place a hard plastic chair mat under your child's work area.

- If your child is old enough, involve him or her in your business. He or she could help you stuff envelopes or put labels on envelopes.

- Be patient. There will be adjustments to be made on everyone's part.

■ Pets

Pets can be a wonderful addition to a home office and can provide company during the day if you work alone. If you take the time to plan ahead, your pet will be more of an asset than a liability.

- If you have a dog that barks frequently, keep it out of your office during work hours or at least while making phone calls. It's definitely embarrassing to be on the phone when your dog sees another dog and starts barking.

- If you have a pet that sheds, take the time to vacuum or sweep your office often. Otherwise, you run the risk of getting pet hairs in your computer, which could damage it, or on your visitors.

■ Make sure your pet has plenty of toys to chew on. I learned the hard way, after my dog chewed two of my computer disks.

■ Consider getting a second pet to play with the first. If you're out of your office or need to concentrate on a project, you'll face fewer interruptions because they will keep each other occupied. (Note: this works well with pets, but the same principle does *not* apply to children!)

TAKING BREAKS

Working by yourself is so demanding that sometimes the thought of taking half an hour for lunch seems impossible. When you work for someone else, there's always somebody around to "hold the fort," and personal phone calls are often a welcome break throughout the day. None of that applies when you work in a home office.

It's important to take time off for lunch, even if you don't eat much. Think in terms of a car. If you keep driving without stopping for fuel, eventually you're going to run out of gas. Take the time to refuel before you run out of energy.

I recommend to my clients who spend hours working at a computer that they buy some computer games, then stop working and play a computer game for half an hour. This gives your brain a rest and can refresh your outlook when you get back to work.

I also recommend taking walks. By physically getting away from your office, you may mentally be able to take a break.

Read your favorite magazine for thirty minutes. Set a timer if you need to.

It's so easy to get involved in what you're doing that you forget to take breaks. Taking breaks throughout the day, however, will actually make you more productive.

BALANCING YOUR WORK LIFE AND HOME LIFE

When you work at home, you are faced with having to mentally switch from work mode to family mode within minutes. You need to strike a balance between your professional and personal lives, even though they happen in the same place. Here are ten ways to find that balance.

1. Minimize distractions. Some people say, "I could never work out of my home because I would have too many distractions." As a rule, don't go to the kitchen to get something to eat, don't turn on the television, don't get distracted by beautiful weather, and don't let yourself get sidetracked by personal activities such as taking the day off to play with friends. However, being able to occasionally indulge in these pleasures during the day is part of the joy of working at home.

2. Know when to stop working. A good friend once told me that she could never have a home office because she wouldn't be able to stop working. When you work at home, you don't have far to go when you get the urge to get one more project finished. If you're single, it probably doesn't matter how long you work, but if you have a family, you will soon hear complaints from all sides.

I used to work every night during the week until midnight. My work was (and still is) so enjoyable that I spent all the time I wasn't giving seminars or meeting with clients in my home office. Eventually I burned out. I took a few days off, and realized when I had a chance to think about it that if I maintained my current pace I would no longer enjoy my business. Now my work schedule is more moderate and I enjoy my work even more than before. I also spend more time enjoying myself outside work, with my family.

When you stop working, really stop. Close the door to your office or close up your desk and concentrate on your family.

3. Don't eat lunch at your desk. When you take a lunch break, leave your office and eat in another part of your home. Changing your scenery and physically removing yourself from your work will help to clear your mind.

4. Schedule regular "dates" with your spouse and children. A freelance artist I know blocks out every Wednesday afternoon to spend with her husband. They play golf or tennis or go out to lunch. They both know that every Wednesday afternoon is their time to play, no matter what else is going on during the rest of the week.

5. Take at least one weekday off per month to play. At the beginning of each month, schedule a day when you are going to stay completely out of your office and do something else. This would be an ideal day to catch up on reading, see a movie you've been wanting to see, or just enjoy the outdoors. Let your answering machine or answering service take your calls. You'll find that taking a day off will prepare you for a month of productive work.

6. Make a list of fun things you've always wanted to do, then start doing them. Maybe you've always wanted to visit the local art museum but never seemed to have the time. Start checking your local newspapers for activities and upcoming attractions. If you have lived in the same city for years, consider taking a guided tour of the city. You'll learn more about your city in a few hours than you had in several years. The point is to keep your horizons open and not let your work consume your life. The activities you engage in will inform your work and enliven your outlook.

7. Use your office only for business-related activities. Rather than go to your office to read your favorite magazine or new mystery, go somewhere else in your home. This will keep you in the mind set that your office is for business and the rest of your home is for your personal life.

8. Don't use other parts of your home for business on a regular basis. If you have a favorite chair where you sit and read or watch television, don't use it for work. After awhile, it will no longer be a place for you to relax and get away.

9. Include your spouse in your business. Even though you may work in unrelated fields, it's always good to get an outside point of view. Your spouse may be able to give you a solution to a problem you've had on your mind for days. The most obvious answer is sometimes not seen by the person closest to the problem. Also, if your spouse understands your work and what it involves, he or she will be less likely to resent all of the hours you put into it.

10. If you and your spouse work together, avoid talking about business after hours. I know many successful business partners who are also married. They tell me that one of the keys to making this arrangement work is to get away from work for awhile and relax. When you're finished working for the day, talk about something other than work.

A word about vacations. If you ever worked for someone else, two weeks may not have seemed long enough for a vacation. Now that you work for yourself, taking two weeks off may seem unthinkable. Do it anyway. At the beginning of each year, block out two weeks when you will go on vacation and treat that time as sacred. Don't schedule appointments during that time, and don't bring work with you if you go away. It's important to recharge your batteries by taking time off.

Time is a valuable resource of which we may never feel we get enough. Technology, however, is working to change all that. There are devices that promise to give us more time, make our lives easier, and put us ahead of everyone else. In the next chapter, you'll see that by means of the latest electronic equipment, the average home office on main street can now keep up with an office on Wall Street.

13 ◪ ◪ ◪

THE ELECTRONIC HOME OFFICE

In order to hold your own with the "outside world," you need to use modern technology in your home office. Although buying electronic equipment can be a major expense, think of it as an investment in your business. For example, buying a new computer may initially set you back financially, but it will probably enable you to be more productive and to make more money in the long run. On the other hand, using outdated office equipment not only makes you look unprofessional, but will cost you in wasted time over the course of a career.

TELEPHONES: MAKING THE RIGHT CONNECTION

The first piece of equipment you need is a telephone. Your phone is your link to the outside world, and it affects how you make a first impression. If you have a phone that sounds as if you're talking into a tin can, the impression you make is an unprofessional one.

■ **Features to Look For When Purchasing a Phone**

- A *hold button* is more effective and more professional than covering the receiver and hoping the person on the other end can't hear you.
- A *mute button* works well in case you have to cough, respond to someone else in the room, or quiet a barking dog without disrupting your conversation. You can still hear your caller, but he or she can't hear noises on your end.
- *Automatic redial* saves time dialing numbers that are busy.
- *Number storage* is used to recall those numbers you dial frequently.
- *Multiline capacity* will help you meet your growing office needs. Think ahead; this is a convenience you may not need now but will appreciate in the future.
- A *speaker phone* allows you to dial without holding the receiver. While you're waiting for an answer, you can keep working. Use the speaker feature only until you get an answer, in that it's rude to place someone on the speaker phone when you're talking.
- *Portable phones* give you freedom to walk around your office or even outside. I know someone who would take his portable phone to the pool in the summer and make his calls from there.

■ **How Many Lines Do You Need?**

You should have separate personal and business lines. You may even want more than one business line. Whether or not you want to pay the cost of installing an additional business line depends on how many calls you currently receive or project receiving, as well as the number of outbound calls you make. If you make calls all day, I recommend two business lines in your office, one for incoming and the other for outgoing.

Consider other equipment in your office with regard to phone lines. If you have a modem, you will need two phone lines: one to make and receive business calls, and the other so that you can be on your computer at the same time.

It's convenient, but not absolutely necessary, to have your fax machine on a separate line. A number of companies make products called fax switches that allow one phone line to do the job of two. Many companies make fax machines that have fax switches built in. I use one line that has both a fax machine and an answering machine. My answering machine gives callers the option of pressing the start key to send their fax or to leave a message at the tone. I also have a separate business line for incoming calls.

When you first open a home office, you may not want to spend the extra money to get a separate business line. However, you probably don't want to keep using your personal line as your business number. In some states it is illegal to do so and could result in a fine. If you add a business line, you'll be listed in directory assistance and in the white and yellow pages of the phone book, which will make it easier for people to find you. If you write an article or receive publicity and no one is able to contact you, the publicity will be of no value to your business.

Arlene, a video consultant, works with people throughout the country. She didn't want to incur the expense of installing a business line, but after several clients told her how difficult it had been to locate her, she finally relented. The money she was saving by not having a separate business line was outweighed by the business she was losing.

Another factor to keep in mind is taxes. If you use your personal line for business, you won't be able to deduct those expenses at the end of the year.

■ Phone Services

Services available from the phone company vary from state to state. Sometimes phone companies will offer specials wherein they will initiate new services for free; at other times, they may charge a start-up fee. Check with your local phone company to see what is available to you and at what cost. Here's a rundown of the features that could be of use to you in your business.

■ *Call waiting*. If you're on the phone and someone else is trying to call you at the same time, call waiting will interrupt you with a beep to let you know you have another call. This is nice because you never need to miss an important call, and it's nice for your clients because they hear a ring instead of a busy signal. The downside of call waiting is that interrupting your present phone conversation can be awkward, although you always have the option of ignoring the other call.

- *Cancel call waiting.* With this feature, you can temporarily deactivate call waiting by punching in a code before you dial. After finishing your call without interruptions, you can reactivate call waiting.

- *Call forwarding.* This feature allows you to forward all of the calls that come to your phone number to another number. If you are going to be working in part of your home other than your office, you can forward your business calls to your personal line.

- *Three-way calling.* This feature allows you to talk with more than one person at a time. It's especially helpful in setting up conference calls so that your home location is not a liability.

- *Tele-branching,* or *remote call forwarding.* This feature allows you to "keep" your phone number if you move. Callers who dial your old number will reach you at your new number.

- *Call hold.* With call hold, by pushing certain buttons you can put your caller on hold even if you don't have that feature on your phone.

- *Automatic callback.* If you've tried to reach someone and keep getting a busy signal, automatic callback will continue to call until the other person's line is free. When the call is completed, your phone will ring; when you pick up your phone, you'll hear the other person's phone ringing. This feature is especially helpful for people who do a lot of phone contact; they can do something else while waiting for their calls to go through.

- *Speed calling.* This feature allows you to preprogram your phone with the numbers you call often.

■ Alternatives to a Busy Line

Call waiting is an alternative to your callers getting a busy signal, but if you receive many calls a day, this feature can go from being a benefit to a liability. It's frustrating to be in the middle of an important call and hear a beep, knowing you must either interrupt your present call or lose the one waiting.

In some states, voice mail may be used to take messages when your business line is busy. If you are already on the phone when someone calls in, the line will automatically switch to your voice mail. You could leave a message explaining that you're currently on the phone and will return the call if the caller leaves a name and number. With voice mail, you can also give the caller several options. For example, if he pressed 1, he could hear information about your services; if he pressed 2, he could receive information from you; and if he pressed 3, he could leave a message. Voice mail may be a service offered by your phone company, and voice-mail boards can be purchased to add onto your computer.

To take some of the heat off your business line, you could use your personal line to make outbound calls and reserve your business line for incoming calls. However, it's preferable to keep your personal and business lines separate for tax purposes. If you have two business lines, you can pay an extra monthly fee to have one business line automatically roll over to the other line if the first one is busy.

■ Buying and Using an Answering Machine

Working from a home office means you probably don't have a staff person in your office all day to answer the phone. How do you answer the phone when you're out or busy?

An answering service is one alternative (see page 181), as is voice mail (above). The most popular solution, however, is the answering machine.

When answering machines were first introduced, many people resented them. They wanted to talk to a "real person" and would hang up if they reached a machine instead. Times have definitely changed. Most people today have answering machines, for both personal and business reasons.

Answering machines continue to improve in quality and in the number of features available. When considering a particular machine, think about the following questions:

- Does it have the capacity to record all of the messages you expect to receive?
- How is the sound quality? Will your message be clear or muted?
- Does it have one or two tapes? I recommend that you buy an answering machine with two tapes: one for your outgoing message, and one for incoming messages. One-tape machines have a major disadvantage: the "beep" at the end of your mes-

sage gets longer and longer as your messages accumulate, to the point where the machine sounds as if it isn't working. People may not wait through the long "beep" or may not leave a message because they think your machine is broken.

- A personal memo feature allows you to record messages for someone within your home.

- Older machines have a beeper that allows you to retrieve messages when you are away from your office. They work, as long as you don't lose or break the beeper. With newer machines, you punch in certain numbers on the phone you're calling from to retrieve your messages.

- A time/date stamp that is heard after each message let's you know when the person called.

- The toll-saver feature lets you know if you've received new messages since the last time you called your machine. It will save you long distance charges because if you don't have any new calls, you can hang up before the machine answers.

- Auto erase is another feature that will save you time and money. If you are out of your office, you can erase messages after you have written them down. The next time you call your machine, you'll hear only new messages.

- Outbound message change lets you change your message from another phone. All you have to do is call your machine and record a new message.

Make sure the message on your answering machine is professional. A cute or clever message is a definite signal that you are not professional (unless, of course, you are a comedian or entertainer). If you don't like recording messages, ask someone to do it for you.

Your message should include your company name, a request that the caller leave a name, phone number, time of call, message, and the best time for you to return the call. Getting the best time to return the call has saved me countless hours of telephone tag.

If you are using one phone line for both personal and business calls, you could answer with your phone number ("Thank you for calling 555-1111"). This sounds professional, yet people calling for personal reasons won't get confused and hang up.

Change your message every few months. Clients who call you repeatedly will appreciate the variety. Irving and Rhonda, partners in a small home-based fragrance company, take turns recording their outgoing message each month to keep it from sounding stale.

Leave your answering machine on at all times. This way you won't forget to turn it on when you leave your office. When I'm not in my office, I leave my machine set to answer on the second ring. When I'm in my office, I set it to answer on the fourth ring. Some answering machines will automatically turn on after the twentieth ring. This could be a good feature if you accidentally turn your machine off.

■ How to Make Better Use of Your Phone

Anybody can use a telephone, but using a telephone to maximum benefit takes a little effort. Use the following guidelines to get the most out of your phone time:

Answer your phone professionally, rather than just saying hello. Answer with your company name, or give a greeting (good morning or good afternoon) and your name. You could also answer by giving your full name. Whatever method you choose, make sure it gives the impression you want.

Answer your phone in a positive tone. You could even smile before you answer a call. The way you think you sound and the way you come across to the person on the other end may be totally different.

One afternoon I met with a friend who works at the Zig Ziglar Corporation in Dallas. As I was waiting for her to come out to the reception area, I heard the receptionist answer the phone with, "Good morning, it's a great day at Zig Ziglar's, this is Joyce." After hearing her answer about twenty calls this way, I couldn't resist asking her how she maintained her enthusiasm. She said that the Zig Ziglar Corporation has a reputation as a motivational company and that's what people expect when they call. She also said that she enjoyed her job and talking on the phone, and that "you never know when Mr. Ziglar is going to call!"

There's a saying that goes, "People like doing business with people they like." In that the first impression you make will probably be through a phone call, make your callers happy that they called, instead of scaring them away.

Do not let a child or anyone who is not willing to answer the phone professionally answer your phone. The one time your six-year-old picks up the phone may be the time a prospective client finally decides to contact you. This one incident could make him or her have second thoughts.

Plan important calls ahead. When you have scheduled a phone appointment and the information you are going to discuss is detailed, send the information to your client beforehand. This will give him or her a chance to review it ahead of time, as well as look at it with you as you talk. Set up your phone appointment for a time when you will not be interrupted.

Take notes as you talk to clients. If you handle a great number of calls, consider using a tracking program on your computer that lets you keep a continuous log of your conversations. Or, grab your personal planner and write in the blank page opposite your "to do" list or in the "client status" section. If you wait until later to write down your conversation, you may get several more phone calls or interruptions and forget what was said or what you agreed to do.

Use a kitchen timer to time your calls. When the timer goes off, wrap up your conversation.

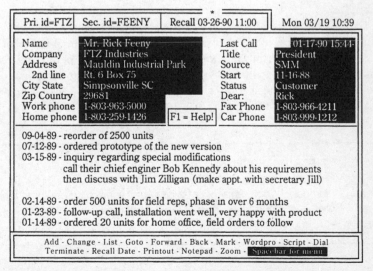

Software programs are available that give you a computerized way to keep track of your client conversations. (Courtesy of Remote Control International)

Don't apologize for putting someone on hold. This will make them feel they've been slighted. Instead, use positive language, such as, "Thank you for holding."

■ Keeping Track of Phone Messages

If you're the only one answering your phone or taking messages from your machine, you don't have to worry about phone message slips. Use either a telephone log or a plain spiral notebook to keep track of messages. Write down the date, time, caller's name, company, and message.

When you use a phone log or notebook, you cut down on the number of scraps of paper in your office, and you have a convenient way of looking up clients' phone numbers. With a running record of both incoming and outgoing calls, you can easily track your long distance calls and calls that should be billed to clients.

If you advertise in various publications or through other media, track the phone calls you receive as a result to see how effective your ads are. This will help you decide whether or not to renew these ads.

You'll also want to keep track of referrals. If a caller was referred by someone, make a note of that person's name so that you can send a thank-you note.

Explain the message system you use to anyone who works with you. If you must use message slips, use only phone message booklets with carbon copies that remain in the book so that you'll have a permanent record of phone calls and phone numbers in case you need them at a later date. The only time you might need to take the originals is if you were leaving your office and didn't have time before you left to transfer the messages to your "to do" list for that day.

QUICK TIP FOR HOME OFFICE PROFESSIONALS

If your credit card offers warranty protection, buy your office equipment on credit. Some card companies will double the manufacturers' warranty up to one year.

PHONE LOG				
DATE	NAME	COMPANY	NUMBER	MESSAGE

A phone log like this one helps you keep track of your work-related calls.

BUYING THE RIGHT COMPUTER

People were once afraid that their jobs would be taken over by computers. Instead, computers have proven to be invaluable to the home office professional. The home office of today needs at least one computer to keep up with all of today's business needs. You cannot be competitive, regardless of your business, without a computer.

When Michelle worked in a corporate office, she never learned how to use a computer because her secretary did all of her typing for her. When she opened her home office, she felt she was computer illiterate but didn't want to spend endless hours learning how to use a computer. She also believed that she could do whatever she needed to do without a computer.

My first challenge was to persuade Michelle that a computer would make her life easier. After I detailed the various ways she could use a computer in her work—and because she was a wedding planner, there were plenty—she was convinced that a computer would help her, but she was still afraid that learning to use one would be too difficult. I suggested that Michelle buy a Macintosh, and after she bought it, I showed her how easy it was to use. Now she is happily computer literate.

Some people are avid Macintosh supporters, whereas others would never consider replacing their IBM-compatible computers. There used to be vast differences between Macintosh and IBM-compatible computers, but with the introduction of Microsoft Windows and other programs, the gap between the two has narrowed.

If you already own a computer and want to upgrade, you'll know what you want your new computer to do. If you've never had a computer, these tips from Ron Baldridge, a computer expert, will help you select the right computer to meet your needs.

- Why are you buying the computer? Do you need to do word processing, desktop publishing, software development, or bookkeeping? You may want to find software that suits your needs and then buy a computer that is compatible with the software.
- How much are you willing to spend? Remember that this is an investment in your business.
- Will you be able to upgrade the computer as your business grows? In time, you may need more sophisticated computer capabilities.

- What type of support is available if something goes wrong with it? Make sure you buy from a reputable source.
- How long is the warranty? Will you have any trouble getting your computer serviced?

If you choose a computer that comes in a unit with a monitor, make sure the size of the screen is comfortable for you. Some people find a larger screen is easier to work with for prolonged computer work. If you buy a separate monitor, you have a wide variety of choices. Check out your options at computer stores, and ask to see various models in action.

Buying a computer is a big decision, but don't go crazy worrying about each piece of hardware and the many software programs available. Talk to friends, buy from somebody you trust, and acquire more sophisticated equipment as you become more experienced.

■ Computer Maintenance

To protect your investment, turn off your computer during a lightning storm, even if you have a surge protector. If you have a modem, unplug your computer and your phone to avoid blowing integrated circuits.

It stresses your computer to turn it on and off throughout the day. However, if you leave it on, you run the risk of burning an image into the screen. To avoid this, install a "screen saver" program. If there has been no activity on your computer, after several minutes the screen saver will appear. All you need to do to bring back the screen is to start typing again or to move the mouse. Another option is to turn down the brightness each time you stop working.

Protect your computer from dust by using a soft nylon dust cover. Protect it from viruses on the inside by installing antivirus programs.

Make sure your office has enough power to handle your office equipment. Otherwise, you may constantly blow fuses or cause power surges.

CHOOSING THE RIGHT PRINTER

Which computer you choose is your first decision, but because you're in a home office, it's not what your clients will see first. What they'll see is the output from your computer. When shopping for a printer, consider the following factors:

- Is it compatible with your computer?
- What is the quality of the printing? Laser printers give the highest quality printing. The print from dot matrix printers ranges in quality from acceptable to excellent.
- What is the paper capacity? The more paper a printer holds, the less time you'll spend having to add more.
- Does it have a straight-through paper feed, or does the paper go from the top to the bottom of the printer, causing it to curl?
- How many pages per minute does it print? Speed isn't everything, but a slow printer can be annoying when you have a lot to do.
- Look at the "footprint," or the amount of desktop space it needs, including the paper tray. Can you accommodate it?
- Will it print in all of the fonts you need?
- Does it have a manual feed for envelopes?
- Does it print in color?
- Will it print on overhead transparencies?
- Is it affordable?

CHOOSING THE RIGHT SOFTWARE TO HELP YOU GET ORGANIZED

There are many software programs available to help you schedule your days, reduce paperwork, and keep track of clients. Before you buy a software program to get organized, consider the following:

- Does it have all of the capabilities you need?
- Will it help you save time?
- Is it easy to use?
- Is it compatible with your daily planner?
- Will it provide you with all of the documentation you need?
- Does it have more features than you will ever use?

Choose software the same way you would choose another product for your home office. Make sure you will be able to adapt it to fit your needs, instead of vice versa. I have included in the Resource Guide at the back of this book a listing of computer magazines that provide reviews of various programs available.

ORGANIZING YOUR DATA

A computer is a great organizing tool, but it creates some organizational challenges.

- Use your computer's hard drive to run your software, and use disks to store your data.
- Use a disk holder to store your disks. Disk holders come in a wide variety of sizes and styles. Keep the disks you use more often within reach.
- When taking disks with you, use a protective case.
- Label your disks clearly. Write the name of the general categories of documents on the label so that you won't have to open each document to find out what is on the disk.
- At the end of each day, back up the information on your hard drive by putting it on disk. Copy the files you used or created that day. This will help you avoid losing valuable documents in the event of a power failure.
- When you're working on a long document, back it up every ten to fifteen minutes. Otherwise, if you have a system error or power failure, you could lose everything.
- Go through your disks once a month and purge the documents you no longer need.
- Give your computer files the same names as the files in your filing cabinet. If you have a hanging folder labeled Correspondence in your filing cabinet, label the directory Correspondence, too.
- Keep the same type of information stored on computer disks. For example, all sales letters should be on one disk; all client information could be on another.
- Protect important disks by storing them in fireproof safes.

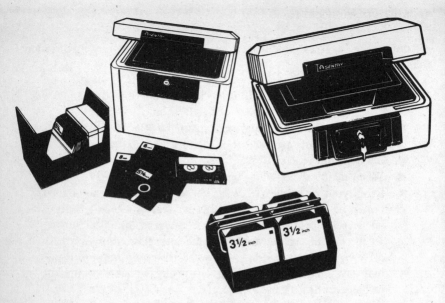

Use a fireproof safe to store important disks. (Courtesy of Sentry Group)

PORTABLE COMPUTERS

If you're on the road more than you are in your home office, a laptop computer will give you access to the information you need when you need it. Most home office professionals don't have an assistant in the office who can give them the information they need, so a portable computer is appealing.

There are four main categories of portable computers.

- Portables that operate on ac current. They weigh from 10 to 18 pounds.
- Battery-powered laptops. They range from 7 to 14 pounds.
- Notebook computers generally fit inside a briefcase and weigh under 6 pounds.
- Palm tops, smaller hand-held computers, measure approximately 6.3″ x 3.4″ x 1″ (closed).

■ What to Look for When Buying a Laptop Computer

Use the following guidelines for buying a laptop:

- Consider the size and weight. If you're going to take it with you when you travel, will you have the room for it and will it be light enough to take with you?
- Make sure that the battery life is long enough for you. The average is two hours.
- Check to make sure the resolution of the display can accommodate the software or applications you plan to use.
- Test the keyboard to make sure your fingers are not cramped using it.
- Make sure the laptop has enough memory for your needs. Some laptops have a hard drive only, whereas others connect to your main computer and allow you to use floppy disks.
- Does the laptop have peripheral capabilities? You may want the option of connecting a modem, printer, scanner, or fax machine.

FACTS ON FAXES

Years ago, we depended on the postal service to deliver our mail. Then there was the option of overnight or even same-day delivery. Now there is the fax (facsimile) machine, which gives us the ability to transmit documents anywhere in minutes.

If you are spending a fortune on faxes (as much as $4 per outgoing page and $2 for incoming), the next purchase for you to consider is a fax machine.

■ What to Look for in a Fax Machine

There are many fax machines to choose from in a wide range of prices. Fax machines are available with an array of features, including the following:

- *Automatic document feed.*
- *Copier.*

- *Automatic paper cutter.*
- *Delayed transmission.* You can preprogram your fax machine to send documents later in the day when phone rates are lower.
- *Document memory.* If your machine runs out of paper, it will save a certain number of pages in memory.
- *Phone number memory.* This feature is used to store numbers you dial frequently.
- *Broadcasting.* With this feature you can send the same document to several locations instead of repeatedly feeding it into your fax machine and dialing the phone several times.
- *Plain paper.* Some fax machines use plain paper. Regular fax paper has a finish that some people find annoying, and images on fax paper will eventually fade. (Hint: you can get around this problem by copying faxes you receive onto plain paper.)

There are also computer boards available that let you use your computer as a fax. Instead of printing out fax messages, you can read them on your screen and print out only those you want to keep in your paper files.

■ Tips for Organizing Your Fax

Use the following guidelines to get the most out of your fax machine:

- Keep your fax on a stand that gives you file space below, or a cabinet that has space in which to store rolls of fax paper. I keep my fax supplies, fax log, cover sheets, instruction manual, and a pen in a cabinet under my fax machine.
- Send fax transmissions after prime time hours. You'll save money on phone line charges.
- Design your own cover sheet, or buy preprinted sheets. *Fax This Book,* by John Caldwell (Workman Press, 1990) is filled with humorous fax cover sheets. If you've attempted to reach someone by phone and he or she won't return your calls, fax-

ing one of these sheets with a message may get his or her attention.

■ Keep a fax log. When your phone bill comes, you'll have a record of the faxes you sent, which will make obtaining reimbursement from your corporate office or charging your clients easier. A fax-activity log book that comes with duplicate log sheets would help you keep track of how much you spend per client on faxes.

■ Instead of a large cover sheet, use small, self-adhesive fax notes. By attaching one of these to your document, you'll save money on air time, as well as fax paper at the other end.

■ Write on the cover sheet (or note) what you are faxing and how many pages there are. This way the person on the other end will know if the transmission was complete.

To save phone line time, use a self-adhesive fax memo or fax label instead of a cover sheet on your fax transmissions. (Courtesy of Avery)

COPIERS

Investing in a copier can save you innumerable trips to the local copy center. Various copiers are designed for home office use. They are smaller than corporate office copiers and are priced lower. The following are the features to look for in a copier:

- *Size.* Do you have room to store it? If it has a moving platen (the surface on which you place your originals), make sure there is enough room for it to move back and forth.
- *Quality of copies.* If the copy quality is marginal, you'll still be spending time at the copy center. Paying more does not necessarily guarantee better quality, so test each machine carefully before you buy.
- *Cost of supplies and maintenance.* If the copier is priced low but the toner cartridges are expensive, you will wind up spending more in the long run than you would at a copy center.
- *Copy sizes.* Do you need to reduce or enlarge copies? Do you need legal- and letter-size copies?
- *Paper tray.* If you make only a small number of copies, it may not matter if you have to hand feed each sheet. If you make multiple copies throughout the day, you'll want a copier with a paper tray and automatic feed.

Technology today is making it easier for anyone to work at home and still communicate with the world. Deciding what equipment to buy and selecting the equipment that meets your needs will keep your business in step with the electronic age.

14 ◩ ◩ ◩

TURNING YOUR CAR INTO A FUNCTIONAL OFFICE

Today your car can be an extension of your home office. With all of the technology available, you can now take care of business from your car instead of having to go home between appointments.

Some people's cars look like a home and an office combined. They have clothing in the trunk, books and magazines in the back seat, and food up front. It takes more than just putting a phone in your car to make it a functional office. You need to set it up logically and without clutter.

YOU *CAN* TAKE IT WITH YOU

Stephen, a sales rep, never knew what materials his clients would want, so he usually guessed. He would throw some sales sheets in the car before appointments and hope they would be the right ones. If they turned out to be the wrong ones, he would send further information later. Soon he noticed that his postal expenses were getting out of hand, and he realized he was spending a lot of time writing cover letters to accompany the additional information.

We set up files in Stephen's trunk with a few complete sets of all the sales information he had. Each month he would replace the sales materials he had given out. Whenever he found he was missing some paperwork a client wanted, he only had to go out to his car to get it. Result: everybody was pleased.

It happens to everyone: you go to mail some documents at the post office and you realize you need to include a note, but you don't have any stationery with you. You have to go back to your office, then back to the post office, and by the time your paperwork is mailed you are behind schedule and thoroughly irritated. Solve this problem by creating a car office kit.

QUICK TIP FOR HOME OFFICE PROFESSIONALS

If you're on the road a lot, be good to your car. Get on a regular maintenance schedule, even though trips to the garage are a nuisance. Preventive maintenance will ultimately save you money and possibly the humiliation of missing an important meeting because of a breakdown.

HOW TO CREATE A CAR OFFICE KIT

Start with a box with a lid, a soft-sided bag, or a briefcase that will stay in your car at all times. Pick a size that will fit in your trunk, on the back seat, or on the floor of the passenger side of your car. Wherever you keep your kit, make sure it's accessible and that it won't slide around or get in your way. In your car office kit, put whatever items you will need, including the following:

- Letterhead stationery and envelopes
- A roll of stamps
- Calculator
- Pens/pencils
- Pad of paper
- Paper clips
- Staple remover
- Small stapler
- Small scissors
- Tape dispenser

- Rubber bands
- Napkins (for those unavoidable meals in the car)
- Change for tolls and parking
- Minicassette recorder for taking notes
- A clear, plastic zippered pouch to hold maps and important documents (car registration, insurance card)

Remember to restock your supplies when they run low.

FILES, NOT PILES

In your home office, you store papers vertically in files, rather than horizontally in piles. The same principle applies to your car. If you don't store papers properly in your car, there's a good chance you'll lose them or that they'll get ruined. Keep papers and sales literature easily accessible and safe by storing them in files or notebooks. You can't bring your filing cabinet into your car, but there are other options that will work.

- A sturdy file box makes it easy to transport files from your home office to your car. It holds hanging folders with interior files and can come with a clear lid to protect your papers. A file stand with wheels is available that you can keep in your home office to hold your file box.

A portable file box with a lid will organize and protect your papers in your car. (Courtesy of trav-L-file)

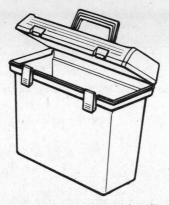

A portable file box is a good way to transport a few file folders. (Courtesy of W.T. Rogers)

- "Milk crate" file holders, sturdy and functional, also hold hanging folders with interior files. They're small enough to store on the back seat or in the trunk of your car.
- Notebooks are an alternative to hanging folders. Store your papers in the notebooks, and the notebooks in a file box or crate.
- A portable file holder works well if you don't need to keep many files in your car. Several companies make small file holders that have handles and snap shut. They have room for files inside and room for supplies on top.

HELPFUL CAR OFFICE ORGANIZING PRODUCTS

When you outfit your car office, try thinking like a major manufacturer. Most manufacturers have special divisions within the company whose job it is to develop products to make our lives easier. They identify an organizing problem and design the ideal product to solve that problem.

Before you buy any equipment for your car, determine what your challenges are. Then find the product that will help you meet that challenge. The following are a few options:

- The Auto Office by Eldon/Rubbermaid gives you a place to store files, your phone, and supplies. It also has a clipboard to be used as a sturdy writing surface.

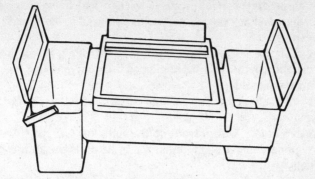

The Auto Office by Eldon/Rubbermaid. (Courtesy of Eldon/Rubbermaid)

A storage clipboard is a car office essential. (Courtesy of Eldon/Rubbermaid)

■ A visor organizer clips to your visor and holds extra pens, change, and any other small items you need to have readily accessible.

■ A clipboard is useful when you need a writing surface in your car. You could use a basic clipboard or buy one that has storage room inside.

■ A little note pad with a suction cup will attach to the inside of your car.

■ A cup holder will prevent coffee spills on your paperwork.

■ A glove compartment organizer is helpful for storing small items.

■ A holder with pockets that attaches to the back of one of the front seats can be used for all sorts of supplies.

■ A trunk organizer will store emergency equipment such as tools, flares, and jumper cables, and will keep them from knocking into your office supplies.

■ Don't forget a trash bag to keep your car from getting cluttered.

■ Keep a spare key to your car in your wallet. There are keys available that are made out of plastic and are as thin as a credit card.

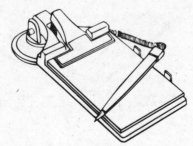

A small note pad with a suction cup keeps paper and pen handy in your car at all times. (Courtesy of W.T. Rogers)

YOUR BRIEFCASE: THE LINK BETWEEN YOUR CAR AND YOUR HOME OFFICE

Transporting papers back and forth from your home office to your car and from your car to appointments often results in lost papers. You need a briefcase.

You will save time and be more efficient if you make the effort to organize your briefcase. Even a state-of-the-art briefcase will work only as well as you organize it.

- Use interior folders labeled To Do, To File, To Read, and To Do on Return. When you get back to your home office, take out all of the folders and sort the papers into their correct places in your home office.
- The Sort-Pal, made by Pendaflex, is a favorite among my home office clients because it makes it easy to transport papers from one place to another. It's ideal for holding papers that need to be copied or faxes that need to be sent while you're on the road. It has six dividers with preprinted labels, and also comes with blank labels so that you can customize it.
- Before you leave for an appointment, make sure everything you need is in your briefcase. You're more likely to remember all of your important paperwork if you make a note on your "to do" list to pack exactly what you need.

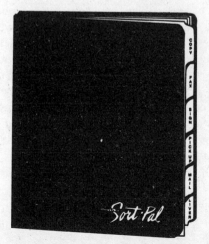

The Sort-Pal from Pendaflex is useful for transporting papers.

KEEPING TRACK OF MILEAGE

If you plan to claim mileage on your income tax, you need to keep accurate records. There are a few ways to ensure you'll have the documentation you'll need in the event you are audited.

- Record your business mileage in the travel section of your planning notebook (see page 86).
- Or, write down your business mileage on the blank page facing your "to do" sheet in your planning notebook.
- Another option is to keep a steno pad in your glove compartment and use columns to record the date, point of departure, destination, and miles traveled.

CAR PHONES

For some, a car phone is a luxury, whereas for others it is a necessity. In some professions, being able to respond quickly to a client may mean the difference between making a sale and losing it to a competitor. In other professions, it may mean the difference between life and death.

My father is a pediatrician, and the joke in our family was that he knew where every pay phone was in every theater, restaurant, and store in the city. Now that he has a car phone, he can't believe how much time he used to waste searching for pay phones. Now when his answering service pages him, he is able to respond quickly and take care of patients immediately. To determine if you need a car phone, ask yourself the following questions:

1. If you have a pager, are you constantly searching for the nearest pay phone?
2. Do you spend more than $30 a month on calls from pay phones? (Don't forget to figure in the amount of money you spend on gas driving around trying to find a phone, as well as the amount of time you spend searching.)
3. Are you unable to return all of the calls you receive each day?
4. Are you missing business opportunities because you're unreachable while you're on the road?
5. Do you have clients with strange hours?
6. Are you out of your office more than in it?
7. Do you travel long distances to appointments?
8. Do you need to be more accessible to clients?

If you answered yes to any of the foregoing questions, a car phone could be a worthwhile investment for you. They make efficient use of "down time" when you would otherwise just be driving around.

■ Types of Car Phones

There are three basic types of car phones: permanently mounted phones, "bag" phones, and hand-held phones. Each fills specific needs.

- Permanently mounted phones are not removable and have three watts of power. Most have an external speaker option.
- The "bag" phone also has three watts of power but is portable. It plugs into the cigarette lighter of your car when in use. You can also purchase a battery that enables you to use the phone anywhere for a period of time. This type of car phone is ideal for people who switch cars often and popular with those who enjoy outdoor sports.
- The hand-held phone is portable, has six-tenths of a watt of power, and is small enough to fit in a briefcase. People often use them when in restaurants or movie theaters or while engaging in outdoor activities.

Car phones have all of the features available with a regular phone, including call waiting, call forwarding, and conference calling (see pages 190–91). You can even program your car phone to ring to an answering service to answer your calls when you're out of your car. There is also call coding, a service that lets you divide your calls by client for billing. Check with local mobile phone companies for the options available in your area. Mobile phone companies often run specials, offering phones for a low price if you sign up for several years of phone service.

A car phone will work for you only if you buy the right one. Visit a few phone sales centers and test the various types of phones available.

QUICK TIP FOR HOME OFFICE PROFESSIONALS

Give your car phone number to only a few people. If many people are able to call you directly, you'll spend more time handling incoming calls than placing outgoing calls, and you'll see an increase in your phone bill. Clients can always reach you by pager, answering machine, voice mail, or answering service.

■ Taking Notes and Maintaining Phone Numbers

One of the problems with using a car phone is that you need a place to take notes as you're talking or when you're finished with a conversation. In order to use your car phone to best advantage, I recommend that you do the following:

- Take notes in your daily planner during phone calls, either in the "client status" section or on the blank page facing your "to do" list. After you return to your office, transfer this information to your computer program or client files.
- Use a phone log like the one in your home office (see page 196) to keep track of your calls.
- Use a notepad that attaches to your windshield (see page 212). Remember to remove the pages you have written on at the end of the day and to transfer the information to your "to do" list or office files. Then toss them.
- Rather than risk your life trying to drive, talk, and write notes at the same time, use a cassette recorder to make notes orally after you've finished talking on your car phone. Remind yourself of what was discussed and what action is needed.

You'll probably keep all of the phone numbers you need in your daily planner. However, there are a couple of products designed specifically for keeping track of numbers you need while you're on the road.

- Electronic organizers (see page 93) will store numbers for you. The Sharp Pocket Auto Dialer has a feature that emits a signal that electronically dials the phone.

■ The "Sun Visor Directory," available through *Hello Direct* catalogue, is a small directory that attaches to the visor of your car. When you move the guide, it opens to the listing you want.

PORTABLE FAX MACHINES

Car phones were seen as a major breakthrough in communication while traveling. Now faxes are viewed as a vital link in up-to-the-minute communication. The popularity of portable fax machines continues to grow. They have made the lives of many home office professionals easier.

Stacy, a real estate agent, calls her office when she's meeting with clients to receive a fax of the latest listings. Her husband, a sales rep, gets the latest prices on his products while meeting with his clients by having the corporate office fax the information to him.

15 ◪ ◪ ◪

GETTING
STARTED

It's easier to say you're going to do something than to actually do it. It's also easy to believe that you really will find the motivation ... tomorrow. The prospect of reorganizing your work life stirs up various emotions.

- *Fear of failure*. What if you can't get or stay organized?
- *Fear of success*. What if you do get organized and become more productive and successful?
- *Anxiety*. Can you accomplish everything you want to? Also, you'll have to get rid of possessions and papers you don't need but are keeping anyway.
- *Excitement*. You're finally getting organized, or achieving a new level of organization.

This mix of emotions is a normal part of making changes in your life-style. It's only temporary, however. After your work life is fully organized, you'll experience joy at living with less stress, and satisfaction from having your business under control.

There are two types of people: those who do, and those who talk about doing. Those who do, plunge head first into every situation and make things happen. Those who talk about it plan far into the future but never for tomorrow. They are always waiting for the right time to make a move—when they get this or that—and never seem to make that move.

You've probably heard people say, "When I open my home office, I'll be happier," or, "When I get a new house, I'll start running my business better," or, "When I land a big client, my business will really take off." There is nothing wrong with thinking and dreaming about the future. The problem arises when you have no clear plan, just scattered ideas. Instead of saying, "When I get . . . ," make a plan and follow it.

CHANGING BAD HABITS

Many people can't get motivated to change their habits until they have a bad experience. For example, if you never have a checkup, you may not discover a medical problem until it is well advanced. If you consistently ignore your car's maintenance checkups, eventually your car will break down and need costly repairs that might have been avoided. After you have a bad experience like these, you might change your ways.

For a home office professional, a bad experience would be losing an account, missing an important deadline, double-booking appointments with two important clients, or appearing unprofessional in front of others. Bad days are part of life, but you're a lot less likely to experience these types of setbacks if you are flawlessly organized.

Don't wait for something to happen to trigger you to get organized. Instead of waiting for that point, do something now to change your bad habits. Although it's easier to continue to do things the way you've always done them, there is probably a better way. Until you try it out, you'll never know what benefits it might bring.

In order to implement changes in your work habits, you need to do the following:

- *Keep your personal motivation in mind.* Everyone has his or her own reason for wanting to get organized. What's yours?
- *Determine why you haven't made these changes before.* What has been holding you back? If you face this problem squarely, it may never trouble you again.

- *Recognize that you have the ability to change.* It's never too late to try something new.
- *Set goals.* The more specific your plan is, the more you will achieve.
- *Apply a new skill every day.* The more you use your new skills, the more effectively they'll work for you.
- *Reward your own good behavior.* Everybody likes positive re-inforcement. When you've earned it, treat yourself.

A representative from a motivational tape company told me about a gentleman who called her and demanded his money back. He had ordered tapes from the company for years and hadn't seen any changes in his life. The woman asked him if he had done anything to make those changes, and he answered no. He thought that listening to tapes alone was going to change his life. You can be like him, and expect that simply reading this book will magically make you organized. In truth, getting organized is up to you.

MAKING A COMMITMENT TO CHANGE

As you can tell by now, I am a firm believer in writing things down. When you write down a task on your "to do" list, you are more likely to take care of it. When you keep track on paper of how you use your time, you can spot time wasters you weren't even aware of before. When you write down your short- and long-term goals and review these goals periodically, you will find that you accomplish more.

The first step to organizing your home office is to make an organizational plan and to commit it to paper. Use the Commitment to Change chart on page 221 to write down what changes you would like to make in your work life and why making them would be beneficial to you. Give yourself a deadline or target date to meet. Put the chart in your planner, or post it in a prominent place in your office so that you can see what progress you are making.

Commitment to Change

Date	Habit to Change	Benefit	Target Date	Date Completed

STAYING ORGANIZED

After you've organized your work life, it's unlikely you will ever return to your previous level of disorganization. The systems you set up after reading this book should suit your needs so exactly that once you get comfortable using them you will be happy to maintain them. Still, to keep motivated, it's helpful to do the following:

- Maintain a network of supportive friends and colleagues whom you trust and whose advice you value.
- Talk to others who are where you want to be. You can avoid costly and time-consuming mistakes by talking to those who have already accomplished what you want to accomplish.
- Keep updating your goals and evaluating your progress. This is best done at regular, predetermined intervals, rather than when the mood strikes you.
- Keep a positive attitude about yourself and your work.
- Listen to motivational tapes. Motivational speakers provide listeners throughout the world with knowledge and inspiration to accomplish whatever they want to accomplish. These tapes give you ways to change the "negative tapes" that you play over and over in your mind. Your "tapes" tell you that you can't do anything right or that you don't deserve to have good things happen to you. When you recognize that you can do more than you thought, the results may amaze you.

There are so many other exciting things to do in life than shuffle paper, react to hourly crises, and increase your stress level. Don't wait until it's too late; take the time now to get organized.

W. Somerset Maugham once said, "It's a funny thing about life; if you refuse to accept anything but the very best, you will very often get it." Getting organized is possible if you combine the direction I've provided in this book with your acknowledgment that you need to make a change, your desire to change, and the action needed to implement change. I wish you the best of everything.

Resource Guide

The following is a list of mail-order companies, publications, and associations.

CATALOGUES WITH ORGANIZING PRODUCTS

Caddylack
131 Heartland Boulevard
P.O. Box W
Brentwood, NY 11717
(800) 523-8060

Hello Direct
140 Great Oaks Boulevard
San Jose, CA 95119-1347
(800) 444-3556

Hold Everything
Mail Order Department
P.O. Box 7807
San Francisco, CA 94120-7807
(800) 421-2264

Reliable Home Office Catalog
1001 W. Van Buren
Chicago, IL 60607
(800) 735-4000

COMPUTER CATALOGUES

Egghead Software
P.O. Box 185
Issaquah, WA 98027-0185
(800) EGGHEAD

Global Computer Supplies
1050 Northbrook Parkway
Dept. 22
Suwanee, GA 30174
(800) 845-6225

MacConnection
14 Mill Street
Marlow, NH 03456
(800) 800-2222

MacWarehouse
P.O. Box 3013
1690 Oak Street
Lakewood, NJ 08701-3013
(800) 255-6227

P C Connection
6 Mill Street
Marlow, NH 03456
(800) 243-8088

Power Up Software
P.O. Box 7600
San Mateo, CA 94403-7600
(800) 851-2917

COMPUTER PUBLICATIONS

Byte
P.O. Box 552
Hightstown, NJ 08520
(800) 257-9402

Compute
P.O. Box 3245
Harlan, IA 51537
(800) 727-6937

Home Office Computing
P.O. Box 53561
Boulder, CO 80322
(800) 678-0118

Mac User
P.O. Box 56986
Boulder, CO 80322
(800) 627-2247

MacWorld
P.O. Box 54529
Boulder, CO 80322-4529
(800) 288-6848

PC Computing
P.O. Box 2886
Boulder, Colorado 80322
(800) 365-2770

PC Home Journal
P.O. Box 469
Mt. Morris, IL 61054
(800) 827-0364

PC Today
P.O. Box 85380
Lincoln, NE 68501-5380
(800) 424-7900

PC World
P.O. Box 55029
Boulder, CO 80322-5029
(800) 234-3498

ADDITIONAL PUBLICATIONS

Entrepreneur
P.O. Box 58808
Boulder, CO 80322
(800) 274-6229

Entrepreneurial Woman
P.O. Box 53791
Boulder, CO 80322
(800) 284-5534

Inc. Magazine
P.O. Box 54129
Boulder, CO 80322-4129
(800) 234-0999

Mobile Office
P.O. Box 57267
Boulder, CO 80322
(800) 274-1218

New Business Opportunities
P.O. Box 58932
Boulder, CO 80322
(800) 274-8333

Success Magazine
P.O. Box 3036
Harlan, IA 51593-2097
(800) 234-7324

HOME-BASED BUSINESS ASSOCIATIONS

American Home Business Association
397 Post Road
Darien, CT 06820
(203) 655-4380

Membership includes monthly newsletter, "Home Business Line."

National Association for the Self-Employed
P.O. Box 612067
DFW Airport, TX 75261-9968
(800) 232-6273

They provide educational opportunities and discounts on business and personal services.

Small Business Administration
409 3rd St., SW
Washington, D.C. 20416
(800) 827-5722 or check your telephone directory for the office near you.

They offer a variety of publications to help you operate your business.

Manufacturer Guide

The following is a list of office product manufacturers. You can contact these companies directly if you are having difficulty finding their products locally or want more information about their products.

BUSINESS CARD HOLDERS

Bates Manufacturing Company
36 Newburgh Road
Hackettstown, NJ 07840
(800) 222-2837

Merrick Industries
690 W. Fremont Avenue
Sunnyvale, CA 94087
(408) 738-2200

Rolodex Corporation
245 Secaucus Road
Secaucus, NJ 07094-2196
(201) 348-3939

COMPUTER FURNITURE

Grolen, Inc.
1100 E. Hector Street
Conshohocken, PA 19428
(215) 825-7213

O'Sullivan Industries, Inc.
1900 Gulf Street
Lamar, MO 64759-1899
(417) 682-3322

Ring King Visibles, Inc.
P.O. Box 599
2210 Second Avenue
Muscatine, IA 52761-0599
(319) 263-8144

Trendlines Inc.
9912 Governor Lane Boulevard
RR3, Box 100
Williamsport, MD 21795
(301) 223-8900

COMPUTER SOFTWARE

Contact Software International
1840 Hutton Drive, Suite 200
Carrollton, TX 75006
(214) 919-9500

Manufacturers of ACT! software.

Intuit
P.O. Box 3014
Menlo Park, CA 94026
(800) 624-8742

Manufacturers of Quicken software.

Remote Control International
5928 Pascal Court
Carlsbad, CA 92008
(619) 431-4000

Manufacturers of TeleMagic software.

COPIER AND/OR FAX MACHINES

Canon
One Canon Plaza
Lake Success, NY 11042
(516) 488-6700

Murata/Muratec Business Systems Inc.
5560 Tennyson Parkway
Plano, TX 75024
(800) 347-3294

Ricoh
5 Dedrick Place
West Caldwell, NJ 07006
(201) 882-2000

Sharp Electronics (see listing under Electronic Organizers)

Toshiba America Information Systems Incorporated
9740 Irvine Boulevard
Irvine, CA 92718
(714) 583-3000

DAY PLANNERS

Day Runner, Inc.
2750 W. Moore Ave.
Fullerton, CA 92633
(800) 635-5544

Day-Timers, Inc.
P.O. Box 27000
Lehigh Valley, PA 18003–9859
(800) 556-5430

Franklin Quest Co.
2200 W. Parkway Blvd.
Salt Lake City, UT 84119
(801) 827-1776

Scan/Plan, Inc.
P.O. Box 1662
Santa Monica, CA 90406
(800) SCAN-PLAN
(213) 829-2888

Time/Design
265 Main St.
Agawam, MA 01001
(800) 637-9942

ELECTRONIC ORGANIZERS

Casio
570 Mount Pleasant Avenue
Dover, NJ 07801
(800) 762-1241

Rolodex (see listing under Business Card Holders)

Sharp Electronics Corporation
Sharp Plaza
Mahwah, NJ 07430
(800) 526-0264

Texas Instruments Inc.
Customer Response Center
P.O. Box 655474
M/S 57
Dallas, TX 75265
(214) 995-6611

FILING CABINETS

Esselte Pendaflex Corporation (see listing under General Organizing Products)

Fire King International
900 Park Place
New Albany, IN 47150
(800) 457-2424

Hon Company
P.O. Box 769
Muscatine, IA 52761-0769
(800) 553-9686

Sentry Group
900 Linden Avenue
Rochester, NY 14625
(716) 381-4900

Venture Horizon Corporation
1231 State Street, Suite 201
Santa Barbara, CA 93101
(805) 564-3441

FILING SUPPLIES

Atapco Office Products Group
P.O. Drawer 639
Kosciusko, MS 39090-0639
(800) ATAPCO-1

Manufacturers of Globe-Weis and Steelmaster products.

Cadence, Inc.
1520 Pratt Boulevard
Elk Grove Village, IL 60007
(800) 621-1092

Eldon/Rubbermaid Office Products Group (see listing under General Organizing Products)

Esselte Pendaflex Corporation (see listing under General Organizing Products)

Fellowes Manufacturing Company
1789 Norwood Avenue
Itasca, IL 60143
(800) 955-3344

Globe-Weis (see Atapco)

Perma Products Company
1346 North Main Street
Duncanville, TX 75116
(800) 527-3198

Smead Manufacturing Company
600 E. Smead Boulevard
Hastings, MN 55033
(612) 437-4111

They offer a "File and Find It" manual, free of charge.

Specialty Wire & Manufacturing Inc.
710 North Railroad Street
Sumner, IA 50674
(319) 578-3427

Manufacture the Framemaster, a file frame that needs no screws to assemble.

Steelmaster (see Atapco)

Trav-L-file
8855 Cypress Woods Drive
Olive Branch, MS 38654
(800) 826-8806

GENERAL ORGANIZING PRODUCTS

Eldon/Rubbermaid Office Products Group
1130 E. 230th Street
Carson, CA 90745–5094
(800) 827-5055

Esselte Pendaflex Corporation
71 Clinton Road
Garden City, NY 11530
(800) 645-6051

They offer a "How to File Guide" at no charge.

K&M Division
525 Maple Avenue
Torrance, CA 90503
(800) 421-1060

Manufacture binders, organizers, and communication boards.

M. Kamenstein, Inc.
190 East Post Road
White Plains, NY 10601
(914) 948-2290

3M Commercial Office Supply Division
3M Center
St. Paul, MN 55144-1000
(800) 362-3456

Tucker Housewares
788 Reservoir Ave.
Suite 155
Cranston, RI 02910
(508) 537-1621

W.T. Rogers Company
2514 Fish Hatchery Road
Madison, WI 53713-2407
(800) 356-8368

LABELING

Avery
Consumer Products Division
818 Oak Park Road
Covina, CA 91724
(800) 252-8379

Dennison
One Better Way
Chicopee, MA 01020
(800) Dennison

LABELING MACHINES

Brother International
200 Cottontail Lane
Somerset, NJ 08875-6714
(908) 356-8880

Casio

(See listing under Electronic Organizers)

Esselte Pendaflex

(See listing under General Organizing Products)

Kroy Inc.
14555 North Hayden Road
Scottsdale, AZ 85260
(800) 776-KROY

They offer a booklet, "Everything You Always Wanted to Know About Organization but Were Too Busy to Ask," at no charge.

Index

A

Accordion file
  for cancelled checks, 169
  tickler file, 100, 104–5
Accountant, 159, 166, 167–68, 169
ACT!, 84, 154, 227
Action, 34
  box, 87, 123
  file, 120
Activity tracking, 171–72
Addresses and phone numbers, 153,
    189, 217
  computerized system, 84, 154
  section of planner notebook, 70, 84,
    89, 154
Advertising, 196
Alphabetical filing systems, 130–34
Answering machine, 15, 36, 185
  buying and using, 181, 192–94
  /fax, 190
  /phone, 42
  where to put, 54
Answering service, 181, 185,
    215
Appointments
  confirming, 178
  recording, 79, 91
  scheduling, 174
  and time management, 179
Articles
  clipping, 149–50, 151
  how to file, 114, 124, 135
Associations, 135
Audit, 167
Auto Office, 210, 211

B

Babysitter, 15
Baldridge, Ron, 198

Bank statements
    computerized balancing, 164
    storing, 168–69
Basement office, 27
Bedroom office, 23–24
Billing notebook, 107
"Bills to pay" file, 115, 120, 122
Binders
    for cancelled checks, 168–69
    filing in, 140
    for receipts, 161–62
Birthdays, 88
Bittle, Jerry, 173
Blotter, 55
Bookcase, 155–56
Bookkeeper, 160
Books, 155–56
    and planner notebook, 70, 85
Boss, being your own, 11
Box-bottom hanging folder, 115, 116
    tickler system, 103
    using, 132, 143, 169
Breaks, 184
Briefcase, 213
Brochures, 151
Broken items, 32, 56
Bulletin board
    how to use, 64–66
    where to put, 45
Business cards, 152–55, 226

C

Caldwell, John, 204
Calendar
    on desk blotter, 55
    and filing, 107
    monthly, 79
    pocket or desk, 91
Callback, automatic, 191
Call forwarding, 191
Callhold, 191
Call waiting, 190–91

Car
    maintenance, 208
    mileage, 86, 169, 214
    office in, 207–17
    phones, 214–17
Card file, 54, 84
Carpet, 39
Cassette recorder, 216
Catalogues, 149, 150, 223
"Catch-all" file, 133–34
Categorical filing system, 130, 135–37
Categories
    for books, 155–56
    filing, major, 125, 128, 134
    for hanging and interior folders, 128,
        136–37
    planning chart for filing system, 142
    for planning notebooks, 70–71
    for receipts and expenses, 160–61,
        164–66
    for sorting papers, 130
    for stacking bins, 63
CDs, 169
Chair, 20, 36
"Charges" file, 120, 122
Cheap tricks
    office furnishing, 43
    storing desk items, 66
Checks
    cancelled, 166, 168–69
    computerized tracking, 164
Child care, 182–83
Children, 15–16, 179, 182–83
    dates with, 185
    and phone, 194–95
Churchill, Winston, 171
Cleaning, 31
    end-of-day, 176
Clear containers, 52
Clients
    filing system for, 126, 131–32
    and office location, 21, 34
    and planner notebook, 70, 80–81

seeing, at home, 13, 16, 19
status sheet sample, 82
where to keep files, 114, 125
Clipboard, 211, 212
Closet, 51
office in, 28, 29
Clutter
avoiding, 32
and buying office supplies, 49
clearing off desk, 53–67
clearing out of proposed office, 29–32
and filing systems, 108–23
and mail handling, 147–49
as time stealer, 180
Color coding, 139–40, 144
Combination machines, 42
Communication
section of planner notebook, 70, 87
sheet, 87
Commuting, 14
Company information, 131
Competitive information, 125
CompuServ Executive News Service,
151–52
Computer, 145
buying, 198–99
cart, 22, 37
catalogues, 224
client-tracking, 84
finance tracking, 163–64
furniture, 226–27
and layout, 20, 22, 36, 38, 44, 45, 55
maintenance, 199
name and address system, 84, 154
phone log, 195
organizing data, 201–2
planning system, 90, 92
portable, 202–3
publications, 224
software, 200, 227
taking breaks, 184
Computer disk(s)
magazines on, 150

organizing and storing, 201–2
storage file folders, 115, 116, 119
Confidential files, 137, 138
Consulting firms, 9
Copier, 227
buying, 206
and layout, 45
Corporate employees, 1–2
receipt tracking, 158, 159
switching to home office, 8–9, 11
Correction fluid, 57
Costs, 50–51
Creative Organizer, 98
Credit cards, 113
business vs. personal, 159
warranty protection, 196
Current files, 113, 115, 124, 127
clearing out, 123
vs. current reference files, 125
setting up system, 120–23, 125
and "to do" list, 148
where to put, 114
Current projects section of planner
notebook, 70, 80
Current reference files, 125, 126, 127,
132

D

Dates
to remember, 88
with spouse and children, 185
Day, organizing, 72–73
Day Runner planner, 95, 97, 227
Days off, 185–86
Day-Timers planner, 96, 97, 227
Deadlines, 174, 176, 181
Deductions, 159, 167
Delegating, 175–76
Denton, Beth, 169
Deposit slips, 168
Desk
alternatives, 19–20

Desk *(cont.)*
  appearance of, 13
  choosing, 39–40
  clearing off, 53–68, 73
  drawers, organizing, 56–57
  inexpensive, 43
  and layout, 20, 36, 44, 45
  no drawers, 57–61
  what belongs on, 54–55
  what to file in, 114, 120
Dictionary, 88
Dining room office, 24–25
Directions, 88
Direct Marketing Association, Inc., 149
Discount office supply stores, 51
Distractions, 18, 179, 185
Dot matrix printer, 200
Drafting table, 45
Drawer(s), 39
  organizing, 56–57
  stuffer, 109, 110
Dress, 13–14, 17
Dresser, 51
Drop-leaf desk, 19, 20

E

Electrical outlets, 18
Electronic equipment, 10–11, 42, 94,
      188–206
  labeler, 120
  name and address holders, 154
  pocket organizer, 90, 93–94, 228
Electronic mail (E-mail), 145
Employees, 175–76
Envelopes, 163
Errands, 174
  bin, 63
Expenses
  computer tracking, 163–64
  filing system for, 160–61
  how long to keep records, 166–67
  receipts, 158–70

section of planner notebook, 70,
      86–87, 89
sheet, 86, 162

F

Family room, 24–25
Fax, 213, 227
  buying machine, 203–4
  -copier, 42
  labels, 205
  and layout, 20, 36, 44, 45
  log, 205
  organizing, 204–5
  and phone line, 189–90
  portable, 217
  receiving, 147
Fax This Book (Caldwell), 204
File box
  with lids, 42, 43
  portable, 209, 210
File cart, rolling, 41, 45, 58, 60–61, 110,
      124
  what to file in, 114, 120
File crates, 40, 41, 42, 124, 210
File drawer
  color coding, 139
  desk, 43, 57, 114, 120
  too full, 144
File folders, 41, 115–19
  See also Hanging folders; Interior
      folders
File holder, vertical, 55
  types of, 57, 58–60
  what to file in, 114, 120
File jackets, 118
File(s), 108–45
  basics of organizing, 127–29
  car, 208, 209–10
  computer, 201
  index of, 128
  and layout, 39
  letter, vs. legal size, 129–30

names, 127, 201
personal vs. professional, 15
planning chart, 142
purging, 126–27, 129
types of, 113–14, 124
Filing cabinet, 228
choosing, 40–42
hanging frames, 57, 127–28
lateral, 41, 44
and layout, 20, 26, 35, 36
what to file in, 114
where to put, 44, 45
vertical, 41, 44, 56, 57
Filing systems
alphabetical, 130–34
in binders, 140–41
for cancelled checks and bank
statements, 169
categorical, 134–37
categories, four major, 125
color coding, 139–40, 144
current, 121–23
finding right type, 130–40
getting started with, 141–42
"how to" guides, 229
numerical, 137–39
and personal style, 5, 9–10, 50, 130
for receipts, 160–61
subcategories, 128, 134
supplies, 228–29
three minute test, 143
troubleshooting, 143–44
types of, 124–45
Finances, computerized tracking,
163–64. See also Expenses;
Invoices; Receipts
Flat files, 34
Floor lamp, 45
Focusing, 173
Folding screens, 22
Forms, 135
Franklin Planner, 94, 95, 228
Frequently-used items, 175

Fun, 186
Furniture, 10, 226–27
arranging, 43–45
choosing, 34, 39–43
Future tasks
in planner notebook, 70, 80
in tickler system, 103

G

Garage office, 27–28
Glove compartment organizer, 212
Goals, 220
for changing habits, 220
section of planner notebook, 70,
81–84
updating, 221
Graphics designer, 13
Grid, 35, 45
Grooming, 17
Guest bedroom office, 21–22

H

Habits
changing bad, 219–20
and productivity, 178, 180
Hanging binders, 140–41, 228–29
Hanging file folders
for cancelled checks, 169
for current files, 120
for expenses, 161, 165–66
how to use, 127–28, 132, 136, 138
labeling, 119, 143
losing papers between, 144
ticker file, 100–4
too many, 143–44
types of, 115–17
Hanging file frames, 57
freestanding, 58, 59
how to use, 127–28
Hard drive, 201
Hello Direct catalogue, 217

Highlighting, 156
Hiring outside help, 175–76
Historical files, 113, 124, 125
    sorting and filing, 126, 127, 132
    where to put, 114, 126
Hold button, 189, 196
Home-based business associations, 225
Home life, balancing with work, 184–87
Home office(s)
    clearing out proposed, 28–32
    layouts, 20–28, 35–39
    location, 8, 14, 16, 18–32
    and nonbusiness activity, 186
    number of, 1–2
    organizing, 2–6, 9–10
    separate entrance, 19
    setting up, 10–11
    tax deduction for, 167
"Hot files," 66, 102–3
Hours, 11–12, 16, 178

I

IBM computers, 198
"Ideas" section of planning notebook,
    71, 81
"Important number" file, 113
"In" basket, 148
Index, filing system, 128, 138
Index card ticker file, 100, 106–7
Information
    handling incoming, 146–57
    and planning notebook, 69–89
Intercom, 16
Interior file folders, 58, 59
    for briefcase, 213
    for cancelled checks, 169
    in current file system, 120
    for expenses file system, 161, 165–66
    how to use, 127–28, 129, 132, 136,
        138
    labeling, 119
    plastic, 129

    problems, 143–44
    for tickler system, 104
    types of, 117–19
Internal Revenue Service (IRS), 86,
    166–67
Interruptions, 12, 15–16, 179–84
Invoices
    filing system for, 137, 166
    paid, 114

K

Kitchen office, 26–27

L

Labeling
    articles, 151
    binders, 140
    computer disks, 201
    electronic, 120, 230
    file drawers, 129
    files, 110, 119–20
    magazines, 150
    papers for filing, 129
    stacking bins, 63
    supplies, 51, 52, 230
Lamp, 54
Laptop computer, 202–3
Laser printer, 51, 200
Lateral files, 41, 44
Layouts
    planning, 34–39
    sample, 20–30
Letterhead stationery, 16, 208
Letters
    answering, 121, 148
    filing, 114, 121
Letter vs. legal size files, 129–30
Library, 155
Lighting, 18, 27, 44
Living room office, 24–25
Long-term planning, 83, 100, 103, 105

Lost items, 179
L-shaped work area, 37
Lunch, 185

M

Macintosh computers, 198
Magazines
  holders, 66, 150
  how to deal with, 149–50
  See also Articles
Magnetic board, 65–66
Mail, 16, 146–49, 179
Mail Boxes, Etc., 147
Mailing lists, 125
Mail order, 149, 150, 223
Maugham, W. Somerset, 222
Meal receipts, 160
Memory, 73
Messages, 181, 193–94
Mileage, 86, 169, 214
Miller, Steve, 178
Miscellaneous
  file label, 121
  sheets in planner, 77, 89
Modem, 189, 199
Money market accounts, 169
"Monthly calendar" section of
    planner notebook, 70, 77, 79,
    89, 99
Monthly receipts, 161
Motivational tapes, 221
"Move it forward" rule, 111, 115
Murphy bed, 22, 44
Mute button, 189

N

Newspapers, 151–52
Night, working at, 173, 185
No, saying, 174
Notebook
  tickler system, 105–6

  for transporting files, 210, 213
  See also Planner notebook
Notebook computer, 202
Notes
  "action", 87–88
  adhesive-backed, 74, 156
  in planner notebook, 71, 87–88,
    89
  seminar, 125
  and "to do" list, 71–72
Numbers, alphabetizing, 131
Numerical filing system, 137–39

O

Office equipment, 10, 18
  breakdowns, 179
  combination, 42
  electronic, 188–206
  importance of having right, 94
  and layout, 20–21, 36, 43–45
Office supplies, 46–52
  basic, 47–49
  buying and finding, 49–51, 175
  and planner notebook, 88
  product manufacturers, 226–30
  storing, 51–52, 124
Often-used items, 38–39, 67–68
Older reference files, 125, 126, 127, 132
"Orders" files, 121
Organization
  beginning steps, 34–35
  breaking into tasks, 44
  four keys to, 33–34
  getting started, 218–22
  guidelines for layout, 38–39
  identifying problem areas, 49
  maintaining, 221–22
  and personal style, 4–5, 50
  products, 49, 223, 229–30
  to-do list as key to, 71–80
Organizing trays or boxes, 57–58
Oversights, avoiding, 73

P

Paper clips, 129
Paper folder, 47
Paperless environment, 145
Papers
  categories for filing, 130
  current, 121–23
  current reference, 126
  historical, 126
  labeling, 129
  older reference, 126
  sorting, 112–13, 126–27
  in stacking bins, 63
  stacks of, 110–11
  storing, 38, 123
  test, 112, 127
  and "to do" list, 73
  transporting, 213
P-A-P-E-R system, 114–15, 146
Parellel work area, 38
"Pending" files, 120, 121–22
Pens and pencils, 54, 57
Perfectionists, 109
Personal items
  calls, 181
  and commerical planner, 99–100
  expenses, 159
  and filing, 113, 126, 127, 132, 144
  keeping separate, 14–16
  magazines, 149
  and planning notebook, 71
  and spiral notebook, 91
  and "to do" list, 75
Pets, 179, 183–84
Petty cash, 170
Place for everything, 53, 174–75
Planning notebook or system, 154, 214
  and color coding, 140
  commercial 90, 94–100, 227–28
  and computer software, 90, 92, 200
  creating, 69–89
  electronic pocket organizer, 90, 93–94

how to use, 88–89
and personal style, 50
and phone calls, 195
and receipts, 163
spiral notebook, 90, 91
taking time for, 176–77
and taxes, 169
tickler files, 90, 100–7
Plastic file folders, 115, 116
Positive attitude, 221
Postal scale, 47
Postal service, 147
Post office box, 16
Price sheets, 66, 88
Printer
  choosing, 199–200
  and layout, 20, 22, 36, 38, 45, 55
Priorities, 72, 74–75, 80, 91, 177
Productivity, 178, 180
Product sample requests, 89
Professional
  appearance, 13, 16–17, 99, 219
  magazines, 149, 151
  vs. personal life, 14–15, 184–87
Projects
  backup documents, 125
  and bulletin board, 64–66
  current file, 121, 122
  folders and subcategories, 128
  filing system for, 135
  large, and stacking bins, 63
  master list for to dos, 75
  and planner notebook, 80
Promptness, 17
Proofreading, 177
"Prospects" file, 120
Purge date, 129

Q

Quicken, 164, 227
Quick tips
  appointments, 178

blaming self, 55
buying equipment, 196
car, 208, 216
cleaning up, 31
equipment, 94
filing, 107, 110, 127, 130, 143
goals, 81
and items used often, 67
motivation for organizing, 35
moving things ahead, 64
office supplies, 49
organizational products, 50
organization planning, 10, 44
paper piles, 60, 92, 112, 123
personal papers, 15, 113
place for everything, 52
priorities, 75
reading, 151
space use, 42
streamlining, 157
"to do" list, 92, 71
"toss or keep" test, 30

R

Reading, 151
Receipts, 158–70
   and CPA, 168
   filing, 86, 135, 160, 163
   how long to keep, 166–67
   petty cash, 170
   and planner notebook, 86
"Receipts-to-enter" file, 160
Redial, automatic, 189
Reference files, 113, 115, 121,
      124
   types of, 125
   where to put, 114, 132
"Reference" section in planning
      notebook, 71, 88
Referrals, 196
Reimbursable receipts, 158–59
Related items, 38, 52, 57, 174

Reports, 114
Research information, 131
Resource guide, 223–30
Retirees, 2
Rolodex, 54, 84
   business cards, 152

S

Safe deposit box, 113
Sales
   information, 125, 151
   reps, 145
   sheets, filing, 135
Scan/Plan, 98–99, 228
Scissors, 57
Screen savers, 199
Secondary work surface, 55, 57
Secretarial help, 9
Seldom-used items, 39
"Selective neglect," 177
Sharp Pocket Auto Dialer, 216
Shelves
   labeling, 51
   and layout, 20, 24, 26, 36, 43, 45
   for secondary desk items, 55
   special, 34
   storage, 51
Shoe holder, 43, 66
Shopping, 35, 50–51
Silverware trays, 66
Small Business Administration, 225
Small items, four-bag system of
      decluttering, 31
Sort-Pal, 213
Space
   needs, 34
   -saving tricks, 19–20
   storage, 52
   vertical, 42
Spare room office, 21
Speed calling, 191
Spell-checking, 177

Spiral notebook
  phone log, 196
  planning system, 90, 91
Spouse, 185, 186
Stacking bins, 45, 51, 56, 110
  and P-A-P-E-R system, 114
  using and labeling, 61–63
Stacking trays, 61–63
Staff files, 121
Stamp moistener, 47
Stapler, 55
Staples stores, 46
Stationery, 47
  organizer, 57, 66
Stocks, 169
Storage, 8, 18, 24
  for backup supplies, 51–52
  and decluttering, 30
  for everyday items, 51
  labeling, 51
  for small items, 43
  tax return files, 167
  for tickler files, 101
Streamlining tips, 157
"Structured flexibility," 177
Style, 4–5, 108–10
Subcategories for files, 134, 135
  planning chart for, 142
Subject dividers, 70
"Sun Visor Directory," 217
Support network, 12, 221
Surge protector, 199

T

Tape dispenser, 55, 57
Tasks
  scheduling, 173–74
  working style, 109
Tax returns
  and computerized expense tracking, 164
  and CPA, 167–68
  and expense records, 86–87, 214

filing receipts for, 158, 159, 161, 168–69
  folder, 161
  how long to keep, 166–67
  and phone expenses, 190
  tips for making easier, 169
  where to file, 114
Tele-branching, 191
Telemagic software, 84, 154, 227
Telephone, 188–97
  car, 214–17
  and layout, 36
  lines, 15, 18, 189–90
  numbers, 89, 153, 189, 217
  services, 190–91
  tag, avoiding, 181
  types, 188–89
  using, 194–96
  where to put, 54
Telephone/answering machine, 42, 45, 54, 55
Telephone bill
  and fax log, 205
  and phone sheet, 85–86
Telephone calls
  incoming, as interruptions, 179, 180–81
  logging, 196–97, 216
  message tracking, 196–97
  planning important, 195
  section in planning notebook, 71, 85–86, 91
  sheet, 85–86
  taking notes, 195, 216
  timing, 195
  and "to do" list, 72–73, 74, 75
  when to make, 173, 178
Temporary files, 137
1099 forms, 169
Three-way calling, 191
Tickler book, 100
Tickler files, 90, 100–7, 120
Time/Design, 97, 228
Time management, 171–87
  challenges and advantages of, 11–12

and interruptions, 179–84
and office layout, 27
types of, 179–80
Titles, alphabetizing, 131
"To do"
 bin, 63
 briefcase file, 213
 current file, 120, 121, 122–23
 stack of papers, 112, 121–23
"To do" list, 63, 64, 76, 89, 213, 220
 and bulletin board, 65
 color coding, 140
 and commercial planners, 99
 and current file, 121, 122–23
 facing sheets, 89
 format, 75–76
 and future tasks, 80
 and mail, 148
 and notes, 87–88
 and paper filing, 113, 115
 and personal tasks, 15
 and planning notebook, 69–80
 and priorities, 74–75, 177
 and selective neglect, 177
 and spiral notebook system, 91
 storing old, 79
 tickler files as, 100–7
 updating, 75, 79, 80, 87
 using, 77, 107, 114, 115
 weekly, 77–78
 wrap-around, 97
"To do on return" file, 213
"To file"
 bin, 63, 114, 123, 150
 briefcase file, 213
 stack of papers, 112, 126
"To read"
 bin, 63, 149–50, 151
 briefcase file, 213
 file folder, 149
 stack of papers, 112
"To sort"
 bin, 63, 148

stack of papers, 112–13, 122–23, 126, 127
"To toss" stack of papers, 113
Travel
 and business cards, 154
 expenses, 166
 and planning notebook, 71, 86
Trays, divided, 56, 57
Trunk organizer, 212

U

U-shaped work area, 36–37

V

Vacations, 186–87
Vertical files, 41, 44, 56
 freestanding, 57, 58–60, 114, 120
Visitors, uninvited, 179, 182
Visor organizer clips, 212
Voice mail, 191–92

W

"Waiting for response" file, 121
Wall clock, 45
Wallpockets, 66
Wall space, 35, 45, 64–66
Warranties, 199
Washington Post, 152
Wastebasket, 66
Wasted time, 3, 12
 chart, 68, 171–72
 and clutter, 29
 and often-used items, 67–68
 and "to do" list, 72
Weekly "to do" list, 78
White board, 65
Work circle, 67, 175
Working alone, 12
Working at home, 7–17
 balancing with home life, 184–87

Organizing Your Home Office for Success

SPEAKING ENGAGEMENTS

Lisa Kanarek gives presentations to corporations and associations. For further information about Lisa's programs contact:

Everything's Organized
660 Preston Forest Center, Suite 120
Dallas, Texas 75230
(214) 361-0556